☝ **W9-BLG-930**

ASHE-ERIC Higher Education Report: Volume 30, Number 3
Adrianna J. Kezar, Series Editor

Understanding and Reducing College Student Departure

John M. Braxton, Amy S. Hirschy, and
Shederick A. McClendon

Understanding and Reducing College Student Departure
John M. Braxton, Amy S. Hirschy, Shederick A. McClendon
ASHE-ERIC Higher Education Report: Volume 30, Number 3
Adrianna J. Kezar, Series Editor

This publication was prepared partially with funding from the Office of Educational Research and Improvement, U.S. Department of Education, under contract no. ED-99-00-0036. The opinions expressed in this report do not necessarily reflect the positions or policies of OERI or the Department.

ISSN 0884-0040   electronic ISSN 1536-0709   ISBN 0-7879-7282-7

The ASHE-ERIC Higher Education Report is part of the Jossey-Bass Higher and Adult Education Series and is published six times a year by Wiley Subscription Services, Inc., A Wiley Company, at Jossey-Bass, 989 Market Street, San Francisco, California 94103-1741.

For subscription information, see the Back Issue/Subscription Order Form in the back of this journal.

CALL FOR PROPOSALS: Prospective authors are strongly encouraged to contact Adrianna Kezar at the University of Southern California, Waite Phillips Hall 703C, Los Angeles, CA 90089, or kezar@usc.edu. See "About the ASHE-ERIC Higher Education Report Series" in the back of this volume.

Visit the Jossey-Bass Web site at **www.josseybass.com.**

Printed in the United States of America on acid-free recycled paper.

Advisory Board

ASHE

The ASHE-ERIC Higher Education Report Series is sponsored by the Association for the Study of Higher Education (ASHE), which provides an editorial advisory board of ASHE members.

This Issue's Consulting Editors and Review Panelists

Executive Summary

College student departure poses a long-standing problem to colleges and universities that attracts the interest of both scholars and practitioners. Approximately 45 percent of students enrolled in two-year colleges depart during their first year, and approximately one out of every fourth student departs from a four-year college or university (American College Testing Program, 2001). These departure rates varied little between 1987 and 2001 (American College Testing Program, 2001). These rates of departure negatively affect the stability of institutional enrollments, budgets, and the public perception of the quality of colleges and universities. Braxton, Sullivan, and Johnson (1997) call this problem the "departure puzzle."

The departure puzzle has been the object of empirical attention for more than seventy years (Braxton, 2000a). During the past twenty-five years, considerable progress on understanding this puzzle has occurred (Braxton, 2000a). Several notable published works speak to such progress (Braxton, 2000c; Braxton, Sullivan, and Johnson, 1997; Tinto, 1975, 1987, 1993). These works focus on Tinto's interactionalist theory of college student departure, a theory that holds paradigmatic status as a framework for understanding college student departure (Braxton and Hirschy, forthcoming). Braxton, Sullivan, and Johnson (1997) assessed the empirical internal consistency of Tinto's theory and found it needed serious revision. Such a recommendation sparked the development of *Reworking the Student Departure Puzzle* (Braxton, 2000c), an edited volume that includes chapters that propose theoretical approaches to revising Tinto's interactionalist theory and chapters that offer new theoretical approaches to understanding student departure.

Understanding and Reducing College Student Departure encompasses the need both to seriously revise Tinto's theory and to propose other theories. We note in this volume differences in the validity of Tinto's theory to account for departure from residential and commuter collegiate institutions. Accordingly, we advance a serious revision of Tinto's theory to account for student departure in residential colleges and universities and postulate a theory of college student departure in commuter colleges and universities.

We engaged in the process of inductive theory construction for both theoretical developments. Inductive theory construction begins with the findings of empirical research (Wallace, 1971). From these findings, new concepts, patterns of understandings, and generalizations emerge. In other words, a conceptual factor analysis of these findings occurs (Braxton, 2000b). This process parallels the open-coding process used in grounded theory construction (Strauss and Corbin, 1990). These new concepts, generalizations, and understandings provide the foundation for the generation or revision of a theory.

We also discuss the implications of these theoretical formulations for racial or ethnic minority students. This effort to understand the manner in which students from different backgrounds experience the college student departure process looms important because the rate of departure for racial and ethnic minority students differs appreciably from those of Caucasian students.

In addition to seeking an understanding of student departure in residential and commuter colleges and universities, we also strive to reduce unnecessary student departure. Toward this end, we provide descriptions of exemplary campus-based programs in the literature that are designed to reduce student departure. We also put forth recommendations for implementation by individual colleges and universities to reduce institutional rates of departure.

What Changes in Policy and Practice Are Recommended?

We advance six conclusions. First, scholars and practitioners should seriously question the paradigmatic stature of Tinto's interactionalist theory and instead should focus on middle-range theories of college student departure. Second, although both of the theories we discuss in this volume seek to explain departure in different types of colleges and universities, both of them include constructs reflective of economic, organizational, psychological, and sociological orientations toward student departure. The ill-structured nature of the problem of college student departure necessitates such a multidisciplinary perspective (Braxton and Mundy, 2001–2002). Third, both of the theories we describe meet three criteria for a good theory suggested by Chafetz (1978). Fourth, the academic dimension plays a significant role in the departure process in commuter institutions, whereas the social dimension performs a predominant role in residential colleges and universities. Fifth, an upper limit on the improvement of student retention rates in commuter colleges and universities exists. Sixth, no template of a successful retention program exists. In addition to these conclusions, we also suggest directions for further research on the college student departure process.

In *Understanding and Reducing College Student Departure,* we also advance recommendations for policies and practices designed to reduce unnecessary institutional student departure. We advance an overarching recommendation and a set of specific recommendations for institutional policy and practice that take the form of powerful levers of institutional action. In the overarching recommendation, we maintain that institutional efforts to reduce student departure should use an integrated design approach. By *integrated design,* we mean that all institutional policies and practices developed to reduce student departure are intentional and require coordination to ensure that guidelines for the development of such policies and practice are steadfastly followed by designated institutional officers. We advance seven guidelines that an integrated design approach should follow.

The specific recommendations for policy and practice that we present take the form of many small levers of action directed toward the goal of reducing institutional student departure. We characterize these levers of action as "powerful" because they flow from research findings reviewed in this volume and adhere to one or more of Tinto's three principles of effective retention (Tinto, 1993). We offer recommendations tailored specifically for residential colleges and universities and for commuter colleges and universities. In addition, we advance recommendations for implementation in both residential and commuter collegiate institutions: (1) *financial aid should be awarded to* students demonstrating financial need; (2) *individual colleges and universities must make commitment to the welfare of their students an abiding concern;* and (3) *institutional integrity should be an enduring concern of individual colleges or universities.*

The marked difference between the departure rates of racial or ethnic minority students and white Caucasian students necessitates the development of approaches to reducing their departure rates. Although the recommendations offered in *Understanding and Reducing College Student Departure* should foster the retention of students from racial or ethnic minority groups, the difference in departure rates suggests the need for additional remedies. Accordingly, we offer the following recommendations: (1) *colleges and universities must enroll and retain a critical mass of racial or ethnic minority students;* (2) *colleges and universities should embrace a diverse student body, reinforced by inviting speakers, holding programs, and conducting workshops that honor the history and cultures of different racial or ethnic groups on campus;* and (3) *colleges and universities should implement Tierney's intervention model for at-risk students (2000).*

Who Is the Intended Audience of This Report?

Academic and student affairs administrators seeking research-based approaches to understanding and reducing college student departure will profit from reading this volume. Scholars of the college student experience will also find this volume of value in defining new thrusts in research on the college student departure process. The theoretical perspectives found in "Tinto's Interactionalist Theory," "Toward a Revision of Tinto's Theory in Residential Colleges and Universities," and "Student Departure in Commuter Colleges and Universities" will fit the interests of scholars of college student departure. Academic and student affairs administrators will find the implications for policy and practice found in "Exemplary Student Retention Programs," "Reducing Institutional Rates of Departure," and "Conclusions and Recommendations for Scholarship" useful to their efforts to reduce their institution's rate of student departure.

Contents

Foreword

Retention of college students remains one of the key challenges and problems for higher education. Approximately 50 percent of students leave higher education—an issue that policymakers have become concerned about. Why is it such an important issue, and why should you invest the time to carefully review this monograph? As funding for higher education diminishes, maintaining students is key to effective enrollment management. Over the next decade, enrollment management will take a more prominent role on campuses, and retention committees will be formed to avoid loss of revenues. In addition, policymakers are setting benchmarks for retention, asking campuses to become responsible for decreasing attrition and promoting students' success.

Although many administrators will first think about retention in terms of funding and accountability, just as important is the moral commitment to students. Once students drop out of college, they may decide never to return, and their life opportunities may forever be constrained. Therefore, student departure is connected to the development of human potential. Individuals who do not continue may lead vastly different lives from those they would lead if they had completed their course of study. Last, as a developed nation, our success has been tied to a large college-educated workforce. Retention is an issue of importance for individuals (future opportunities), for institutions (financial success, accountability, and moral commitment to a supportive environment), and for the nation that strives to develop a workforce and citizenry to support the future. Few issues could be judged so important to the future of higher education and society.

Another reason that retention has taken on such prominence is a change in philosophy about our responsibility to students. Previously if students dropped out, it was related to their failure, because students had different abilities. Within a talent development model, which has become more prevalent on college campuses, it is believed that all students can succeed with the proper support. Retention is about developing a climate that is conducive to students as well as helping students to make appropriate choices that make them successful.

Retention has received a great deal of attention in the literature and from researchers. Yet it is a complex problem and has been labeled the "departure puzzle" by Braxton, Sullivan, and Johnson (1997). Therefore, a book that summarizes the research from the last thirty years is needed to help professionals understand how to examine and develop solutions for their campuses. This book contributes to our knowledge in several important ways. It synthesizes the various critiques of early models of retention that were developed among white, affluent 18- to 22-year-olds on residential campuses that had limited generalizability and applicability. Over the last thirty years, the early retention models have been challenged and revised several times. In addition, this book proposes new models for nonresidential students and students from diverse backgrounds. One of the major strengths of the monograph is that it acknowledges that there are still many gaps in our understanding that need examination. Any complex problem will need to be explored as new challenges and issues emerge. This book does not suggest that we will ever finally figure out the retention puzzle, but we can become as informed as possible and make evidence-based decisions for improving campus environments and meeting our obligations to individuals and the nation.

Adrianna J. Kezar
Series Editor

The Ill-Structured Problem
of College Student Departure

COLLEGE STUDENT DEPARTURE poses a long-standing problem to colleges and universities that attracts the interest of both scholars and practitioners. Approximately 45 percent of students enrolled in two-year colleges depart during their first year, and approximately one out of every fourth student departs from a four-year college or university (American College Testing Program, 2001). These departure rates varied little between 1987 and 2001 (American College Testing Program, 2001). These rates of departure negatively affect the stability of institutional enrollments, budgets, and the public perception of the quality of colleges and universities. Braxton, Sullivan, and Johnson (1997) call this problem the "departure puzzle."

The departure puzzle greatly interests scholars and practitioners for different reasons. Practitioners express an interest in solving this puzzle to manage the enrollments of their colleges and universities. This puzzle intrigues scholars because departure not only is a problem worthy of attention in its own right but also offers a window on the nature of the college student experience (Braxton, Sullivan, and Johnson, 1997). Through this window, a better understanding of the student college choice process and the effects of college on students may result. Moreover, the considerable energy expended by high school students, their parents, high school counselors, and college admissions officers in the college selection process also makes college student departure a puzzling phenomenon (Braxton, Sullivan, and Johnson, 1997).

The departure puzzle has been the object of empirical attention for more than seventy years (Braxton, 2000a). During the past twenty-five years, considerable progress on understanding this puzzle has occurred (Braxton, 2000a).

Several notable published works speak to such progress (Braxton, 2000c; Braxton, Sullivan, and Johnson, 1997; Tinto, 1975, 1986, 1993). These works focus on Tinto's interactionalist theory of college student departure, a theory that holds paradigmatic status as a framework for understanding college student departure as indexed in more than 775 citations to his theoretical work (Braxton and Hirschy, forthcoming). Tinto (1975) proposed his foundational theory of college student departure, offered revisions to his theory, and also developed some principles for effective retention programs and implementation of such programs (Tinto, 1993). Braxton, Sullivan, and Johnson (1997) assessed the empirical internal consistency of Tinto's theory and found it in need of serious revision. Such a recommendation sparked the development of *Reworking the Student Departure Puzzle* (Braxton, 2000c), an edited volume that includes chapters proposing theoretical approaches to revising Tinto's interactionalist theory and chapters offering new theoretical approaches to understanding student departure.

This volume embraces the need both to seriously revise Tinto's theory and to propose other theories. Such work proceeds along the lines of differences in the validity of Tinto's theory to account for departure from residential and commuter collegiate institutions. The next chapter, "Tinto's Interactionalist Theory," offers an extensive discussion of such differences and provides a foundation for two of the four primary purposes of this volume. These two major purposes center on the advancement of a serious revision of Tinto's theory to account for student departure from residential collegiate institutions and the development of a theory to explain student departure from commuter colleges and universities.

Economic, organizational, psychological, and sociological conceptual orientations undergird both theoretical formulations. A multitheoretical approach is needed because college student departure is best characterized as an ill-structured problem (Braxton and Mundy, 2001–2002). Ill-structured problems defy a single solution and require a number of possible solutions that may not alleviate the problem (Kitchener, 1986; Wood, 1983).

We also discuss the implications of these theoretical formulations for racial or ethnic minority students. This attempt to understand the ways in which students from different backgrounds experience the college student departure process looms important, because in recent years, racial and ethnic minority student patterns of college attendance and degree attainment in the United States have changed profoundly. In 2001, the U.S. Department of Education (2002) reported that African American students, Hispanic students, Asian or Pacific Islander students, and American Indian or Alaskan Native students constituted approximately 28 percent of the total college enrollment for degree-granting institutions. Also according to the U.S. Department of Education (2002), the number of racial and ethnic minority students who were awarded degrees increased dramatically between 1976 and 2000, representing 22.5 percent of all bachelor's degrees conferred to U.S. citizens.

Even with these gains in higher education enrollment and degrees awarded, which have proved to be beneficial to the students and the broader society, the rate of departure for racial and ethnic minority students differs appreciably from those of Caucasian students. Specifically, the six-year rate of departure for Caucasian students is 39.3 percent as contrasted with a rate of 53.4 percent for Hispanic students and a rate of 60.4 percent for African American students who entered a four-year college immediately after high school graduation (Porter, 1990; Tinto, 1993).

In addition to seeking further understanding of the departure puzzle, we also offer approaches to reduce institutional rates of student departure. Descriptions of exemplary campus-based programs designed to reduce student departure exist in the literature. A review of such exemplary programs is much needed. The third purpose of this volume is to address this need. This volume's fourth purpose also concentrates on reducing institutional rates of departure by advancing an overarching recommendation and specific recommendations for implementation by individual colleges and universities.

We limit our theoretical developments to papers presented at annual meetings of scholarly and professional associations, book chapters, and articles published in refereed journals. We restrict our work to such peer-reviewed studies, as peer review provides some confidence in the scholarly quality of these studies. Such confidence stems from the assumption that scholars knowledgeable about the topic of research make assessments based on the quality of the research and its contribution to knowledge (Anderson and Louis, 1991).

The terms *student departure* and *student withdrawal* are used interchangeably in this volume, as are the terms *student retention* and *student persistence.* Although we use these terms as synonyms, we do not take the stance that the onus of retention or persistence rests with the individual student. Instead, we view the departure process as an interaction between the individual student and the college or university attended.

Overview of the Volume

In addition to an introductory and a concluding chapter, the structure of this volume consists of two parts—theoretical frameworks and implications for policy and practice. Such an organization facilitates the reader's use of this volume. The three chapters comprising the theoretical frameworks concentrate on enhancing our understanding of the college student departure process. Scholars of higher education will find these chapters useful in their research. Specifically, the first of these three chapters, "Tinto's Interactionalist Theory," describes this theory and assesses its empirical validity. The next chapter formulates a revision of Tinto's theory to account for student departure from residential colleges and universities, and the third chapter of this set formulates a theory of student departure from commuter colleges and universities.

The second part, containing implications for policy and practice, consists of two chapters focusing on the reduction of institutional rates of student departure. One of these two chapters, "Exemplary Student Retention Programs," describes institutional programs designed to reduce student attrition. The other chapter, "Reducing Institutional Rates of Departure," offers recommendations that assume the form of powerful levers for institutional acts directed toward reducing institutional rates of unnecessary student departure. Practitioners will find these two chapters particularly helpful.

The last chapter of this volume, "Conclusions and Recommendations for Scholarship," advances six conclusions derived from the literature and research findings reviewed and theoretical formulations offered in this volume. This chapter also advances four general and eight specific recommendations for further scholarship on the student departure puzzle. We also proffer some closing thoughts.

Intended Audience

Academic and student affairs administrators seeking research-based approaches to understanding and reducing college student departure will profit from reading this volume. Administrators will particularly benefit from reading the chapters in the second part. Scholars of the college student experience will find the chapters in the first part and the concluding chapter of this volume of value in delineating new research thrusts on the college student departure process.

Tinto's Interactionalist Theory

THIS CHAPTER FOCUSES on Tinto's interactionalist theory, a theory with a sociological conceptual orientation. Because of the paradigmatic stature of Tinto's theory (Braxton and Hirschy, forthcoming; Braxton, Sullivan, and Johnson, 1997), we devote a chapter to it. Paradigmatic status connotes the considerable consensus among scholars of college student departure concerning the potential validity of Tinto's theory. Such consensus manifests itself in the vast number of citations (more than 775) to Tinto's foundational expression (1975) of his theory (Braxton and Hirschy, forthcoming). We assume consensus, because scholars extensively test and cite Tinto's theory (Braxton, Sullivan, and Johnson, 1997). Although Tinto's theory has paradigmatic stature, empirical tests of it show mixed support (Braxton, Sullivan, and Johnson, 1997).

This chapter reviews the formulations of Tinto's theory. It also reviews an extensive empirical assessment of its validity and suggests explanations for some unanticipated findings.

Tinto's Interactionalist Theory

Tinto views student departure as a longitudinal process that occurs because of the meanings the individual student ascribes to his or her interactions with the formal and informal dimensions of a given college or university (Braxton, Sullivan, and Johnson, 1997; Tinto, 1986, 1993). Such interactions occur between the individual student and the academic and social systems of a college or university.

More specifically, Tinto (1975) posits that various individual characteristics (for example, family background, individual attributes, and precollege schooling experiences) that students possess as they enter college directly influence their departure decisions, as well as their initial commitments to the institution and to the goal of college graduation. Initial commitment to the institution and initial commitment to the goal of graduation influence the level of a student's integration into the academic and social systems of the college or university (see Figure 1).

According to Tinto (1975, p. 104), academic integration consists of structural and normative dimensions. Structural integration entails the meeting of explicit standards of the college or university, whereas normative integration pertains to an individual's identification with the beliefs, values, and norms inherent in the academic system.

FIGURE 1
Tinto's Interactionalist Model of Student Persistence

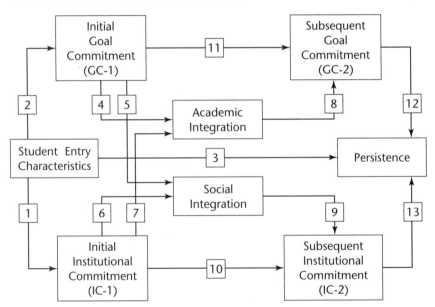

Note: The arrows represent the thirteen testable propositions. The numbers correspond to the propositions listed in "Tinto's Interactionalist Theory."
SOURCE: Adapted from Tinto, 1975.

Social integration pertains to the extent of congruency between the individual student and the social system of a college or university. Tinto holds that social integration occurs both at the level of the college or university and at the level of a subculture of an institution (Tinto, 1975, p. 107). Social integration reflects the student's perception of his or her degree of congruence with the attitudes, values, beliefs, and norms of the social communities of a college or university.

Tinto postulates that academic and social integration influence a student's subsequent commitments to the institution and to the goal of college graduation. The greater the student's level of academic integration, the greater the level of subsequent commitment to the goal of college graduation. Moreover, the greater the student's level of social integration, the greater the level of subsequent commitment to the focal college or university (Tinto, 1975, p. 110). The student's initial levels of commitments—institutional and graduation goal—also influence his or her levels of subsequent commitments. In turn, the greater the levels of both subsequent institutional commitment and commitment to the goal of college graduation, the greater the likelihood the individual will persist in college.

Moreover, Tinto carefully points out that his theory accounts for voluntary student departure (1975). He also stresses that his theory strives to explain the departure process within a given college or university and "is not a systems model of departure" (Tinto, 1993, p. 112).

The above formulations of Tinto's 1975 theoretical statement yield thirteen testable propositions (Braxton, Sullivan, and Johnson, 1997). For Propositions 1 to 7, Tinto does not indicate a direction (positive or negative) for the hypothesized influence, whereas he specifies a positive direction for Propositions 8 to 13 (Braxton, Sullivan, and Johnson, 1997). The thirteen propositions are as follows:

1. Student entry characteristics affect the level of initial commitment to the institution.
2. Student entry characteristics affect the level of initial commitment to the goal of graduation from college.
3. Student entry characteristics directly affect the student's likelihood of persistence in college.

4. Initial commitment to the goal of graduation from college affects the level of academic integration.

5. Initial commitment to the goal of graduation from college affects the level of social integration.

6. Initial commitment to the institution affects the level of social integration.

7. Initial commitment to the institution affects the level of academic integration.

8. The greater the degree of academic integration, the greater the level of subsequent commitment to the goal of graduation from college.

9. The greater the degree of social integration, the greater the level of subsequent commitment to the institution.

10. The initial level of institutional commitment affects the subsequent level of institutional commitment.

11. The initial level of commitment to the goal of graduation from college affects the subsequent level of commitment to the goal of college graduation.

12. The greater the level of subsequent commitment to the goal of graduation from college, the greater the likelihood of student persistence in college.

13. The greater the level of subsequent commitment to the institution, the greater the likelihood of student persistence in college.

These propositions and their relationship are depicted in Figure 1. Propositions 3, 12, and 13 are important to the explanatory power of Tinto's theory because they posit a direction influence on departure (Braxton, Sullivan, and Johnson, 1997). However, we assert that the validity of Tinto's interactionalist theory hinges on strong empirical backing for Propositions 8 and 9. Without strong empirical affirmation for the role of either academic or social integration in the departure process, the underpinnings of Tinto's interactionalist theory come into question. Serious questions emerge about the influence of the outcomes of the interactions a student makes with the academic or social communities of a college or university in the student departure process.

Tinto offers clarifications and refinements of his 1975 foundational set of formulations. This set of refinements (Tinto, 1982, 1986) culminates in a formal revision of his theory appearing in *Leaving College: Rethinking the Causes and Cures of Student Attrition* (Tinto, 1987, 1993). The revisions in the 1975 formulations include delineating financial resources as part of the attributes or characteristics with which a student enters college and an acknowledgment of the role communities external to the institution play in the departure decisions of college students. Family, work, and community represent such external commitments that may influence student departure decisions (Tinto, 1993).

An Empirical Assessment of Tinto

The thirteen testable propositions delineated above are logically interrelated and, as a set, seek to account for individual student departure. Thus, empirical internal consistency looms important to the validity of this theory. The extent to which each of the thirteen propositions receives empirical backing provides the basis for an appraisal of the empirical internal consistency of this theory (Braxton, Sullivan, and Johnson, 1997). Nevertheless, as we asserted above, the validity of Tinto's theory depends on strong empirical affirmation for Propositions 8 and 9, the propositions essential to the interactionalist perspective. Strong empirical backing for Propositions 3, 12, and 13 is also important.

Braxton, Sullivan, and Johnson (1997) assessed the degree of empirical confirmation for each of these thirteen propositions of Tinto's 1975 theoretical statements. This assessment was conducted on the 1975 version of this theory rather than the 1987 and 1993 revised theory because, as of 1997, only two studies tested constructs unique to the 1987 and 1993 versions (Allen and Nelson, 1989; Pavel, 1991). As indicated above, only student financial resources and the influence of external commitments were additions to the 1975 model. The key formulations that define Tinto's theory as interactionalist reside in the 1975 formulations.

The magnitude of support for each proposition was appraised by Braxton, Sullivan, and Johnson using the "box score" method. The percentage of tests of a given proposition that affirm that proposition provides the basis for the box score for each of the thirteen propositions. Strong empirical support was allocated to a proposition if 66 percent or more of three or more tests of that proposition yielded statistically significant affirmation. If between 34 percent and 65 percent of three or more tests of a proposition produced statistically significant backing, then "moderate" support was accorded to that proposition. Weak empirical support was ascribed to those propositions for which 33 percent or less of three or more tests of that proposition produced statistically significant and confirming results. Propositions that were tested one or two times were classified as having indeterminate support, because subsequent tests might confirm or fail to confirm the focal proposition.

The replication of research findings constitutes a cornerstone of social science research. Confidence in the veracity of findings results from replications. Accordingly, we support the use of the box score approach and the percentage of tests affirming a given proposition in a statistically significant way, as it provides a method for assessing the replicability of tests of a given proposition. Other ways of assessing support for a proposition such as the magnitude of the effects observed or the scope of a study (for example, a large national sample) fail to address the replication of findings.

Braxton, Sullivan, and Johnson restricted their appraisal of support for these propositions to tests that included only measures of Tinto's constructs judged as having face validity (p. 110). Face validity was determined by using Tinto's theoretical formulations. They also confined their assessments to tests of a given proposition that employed statistical methods that estimate the independent or net influence of a proposition above and beyond the influence of other constructs that may influence student departure. Put differently, the possible effects of other constructs that might influence departure were statistically controlled. These tests used such statistical techniques as path analysis, multiple linear regression, LISREL, and logistic regression (Braxton, Sullivan, and Johnson, 1997, p. 113). Thus, Braxton, Sullivan, and Johnson based their appraisals of support on rigorous tests of each of the thirteen propositions.

Although Braxton, Sullivan, and Johnson assessed the extent of empirical backing for the thirteen propositions using tests conducted in multi-institutional samples, we describe in this chapter the extent of support only for tests conducted using single-institutional samples. We do so to be consistent with Tinto's assertion (1993, p. 112) that his theory seeks to explain student departure within a given college or university and that it is not intended to explain systems departure.

Propositions Receiving Strong Support

The appraisal of empirical support for the thirteen propositions conducted by Braxton, Sullivan, and Johnson transpired on an aggregate level, by institutional type and by student groups. This approach permits a consideration of whether scholars may view Tinto's interactionalist theory as a grand theory to account for student departure or a middle-range theory that explains student departure in a particular type of college or university or for particular groups of students.

General Support

At an aggregate level, five of these thirteen propositions receive strong empirical backing (Braxton, Sullivan, and Johnson, 1997): Propositions 1, 9, 10, 11, and 13 (see Figure 2). Four of these five propositions are logically connected. A narrative statement of these four robustly supported and logically related propositions takes the following form. Students enter college with various

FIGURE 2
Five Strongly Supported Propositions of Tinto's Interactionalist Model, Aggregate Support

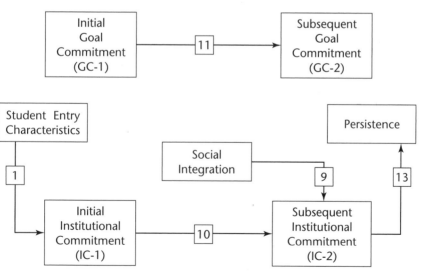

Note: The arrows represent the thirteen testable propositions. The numbers correspond to the propositions listed in "Tinto's Interactionalist Theory."

characteristics that influence their initial level of commitment to the college or university that they chose to attend (Proposition 1). This initial level of institutional commitment also affects their subsequent commitment to the institution (Proposition 10). Social integration also affects subsequent institutional commitment. The greater a student's degree of social integration, the greater his or her subsequent commitment to the institution (Proposition 9). The greater the degree of a student's subsequent commitment to the institution, the greater his or her likelihood of persisting in college (Proposition 13).

Braxton, Sullivan, and Johnson (1997) conclude that, at an aggregate level, partial support for Tinto's theory springs from the strong empirical backing of these five propositions. Moreover, Proposition 9, a proposition pivotal to the validity of the interactionalist underpinnings of Tinto's theory, garners such strong backing. In addition, Proposition 13 also receives robust empirical confirmation.

Tests of Proposition 8, however, receive modest empirical backing. This proposition includes the construct of academic integration, a construct pivotal to the interactionalist underpinnings of Tinto's theory. Because of its importance to the validity of Tinto's theory, Braxton and Lien (2000) assessed the extent of empirical backing for the influence of academic integration on subsequent institutional commitment and on student departure. These possible relationships represent other ways academic integration may influence the student departure process (Braxton and Lien, 2000). They used the same methodology and percentage of tests to assess the extent of empirical backing as Braxton, Sullivan, and Johnson (1997).

This assessment also discerned modest empirical support for the influence of academic integration on subsequent institutional commitment and on student departure. At the aggregate level, the viability of academic integration as a core construct in Tinto's theory continues to plague the validity of his theory.

Support by Institutional Type
Braxton, Sullivan, and Johnson also appraised the extent of empirical support for the thirteen propositions of Tinto's theory by institutional type. The types of colleges and universities included in this assessment were residential

universities, commuter universities, liberal arts colleges, and two-year colleges.

Liberal Arts Colleges.   Although liberal arts colleges represented an a priori institutional category, Braxton, Sullivan, and Johnson (1997) identified no tests of the thirteen propositions for them. Thus, empirical support for the validity of Tinto's theory in liberal arts colleges remains an open question for research.

Residential Universities.   Strong empirical support obtains for five of the thirteen propositions in residential universities (Braxton, Sullivan, and Johnson, 1997): Propositions 5, 9, 10, 11, and 13 (see Figure 3). Four of these propositions hold a logical connection with one another. These four propositions assume the following form: the initial commitment to the goal of graduation

FIGURE 3
Five Strongly Supported Propositions of Tinto's Interactionalist Model in Residential Colleges and Universities

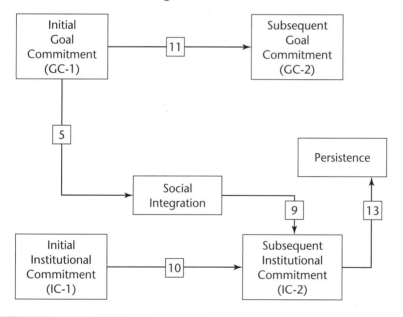

Note: Arrows indicate strongly supported propositions. The numbers correspond to the propositions listed in "Tinto's Interactionalist Theory."
SOURCE: Adapted from Braxton, Sullivan, and Johnson, 1997.

from college affects the level of social integration (Proposition 5). Social integration, in turn, positively affects subsequent institutional commitment (Proposition 9). Initial commitment to the institution also influences subsequent institutional commitment (Proposition 10). The greater the level of subsequent commitment to the institution, the greater the likelihood of student persistence in college (Proposition 13). Figure 3 graphically portrays these propositions and their interrelationships. As a consequence, Braxton, Sullivan, and Johnson (1997) conclude that Tinto's theory receives partial support in residential universities.

The predicted influence of academic integration on subsequent commitment to the goal of college graduation in Tinto's theory, however, garners modest empirical support. Possible linkages between academic integration and subsequent institutional commitment and student departure also receive modest empirical backing (Braxton and Lien, 2000). As a consequence, the role played by academic integration in residential universities remains problematic in residential universities. Accordingly, fundamental questions about the usefulness of this construct in accounting for student departure in residential universities spring from these assessments.

Nevertheless, the four logically interrelated propositions that benefit from strong empirical backing in residential universities provide the foundation for a serious revision of Tinto's theory. Such revisions would apply to residential universities and would recognize the centrality of social integration in its formulations.

Commuter Universities.   In contrast to residential universities where five propositions garner robust empirical support, only two propositions receive such support in commuter universities (Braxton, Sullivan, and Johnson, 1997). These two propositions, which are graphically depicted in Figure 4, are logically interrelated and take the following narrative form: student entry characteristics affect the level of initial commitment to the institution, and the initial level of commitment to the institution affects the subsequent level of commitment to the institution. Social integration and its hypothesized influence on subsequent institutional commitment, however, garner modest backing. Tinto's anticipated influence of academic integration on subsequent

FIGURE 4
Two Strongly Supported Propositions of Tinto's Interactionalist Model in Commuter Institutions

Note: Arrows indicate strongly supported propositions.
SOURCE: Adapted from Braxton, Sullivan, and Johnson, 1997.

commitment to the goal of graduation from college also receives modest empirical confirmation (Braxton, Sullivan, and Johnson, 1997).

Moreover, Braxton and Lien (2000) appraised the extent of empirical backing for the possible influence of academic integration on student departure in commuter universities. Their appraisal identified modest confirmation of this plausible linkage, but they identify strong empirical backing for the relationship between academic integration and subsequent institutional commitment in commuter collegiate institutions.

Taken together, this configuration of support for the propositions of Tinto's theory lacks internal consistency, thereby suggesting that his theory lacks explanatory power in commuter institutional settings. Nevertheless, those propositions identified above as receiving strong affirmation are included in a theory of student departure in commuter colleges and universities described in a subsequent chapter of this volume.

Two-Year Colleges. In two-year colleges, only one of Tinto's thirteen propositions garners robust empirical affirmation (Braxton, Sullivan, and Johnson, 1997): student entry characteristics directly affect the likelihood of students' persistence in college. The remaining twelve propositions, however, either received indeterminate support or were not the object of empirical testing. Likewise, indeterminate support obtains for the possible relationship between academic integration and subsequent institutional commitment, whereas the possible linkage between academic integration and departure receives modest empirical support (Braxton and Lien, 2000). Given this configuration of support, the explanatory power of Tinto's theory to account for student departure in two-year colleges remains undetermined and open to empirical treatment.

Support Across Student Racial or Ethnic Groups

Braxton, Sullivan, and Johnson (1997) report that none of the thirteen propositions of Tinto's theory were tested using different racial or ethnic minority groups within single institutional samples. They indicate, however, that one proposition receives strong empirical backing for Caucasian male and female students; that is, student entry characteristics affect the likelihood of persistence in college. Nevertheless, the validity of Tinto's theory to account for student departure across different racial or ethnic groups remains an open question for scholars to pursue.

Explanations for Unanticipated Academic Integration Findings

Although strong empirical backing exists for the relationship between academic integration and subsequent institutional commitment in commuter universities, other propositions related to academic integration are not strongly supported. For example, the hypothesized positive influence of academic integration and subsequent commitment to the goal of college graduation (Braxton, Sullivan, and Johnson, 1997) and the possible linkages between academic integration and subsequent institutional commitment and student departure fail to garner strong empirical backing (Braxton and Lien, 2000). Such failure requires the development of possible explanations. The centrality of the academic experience to college attendance and the critical importance of academic integration and its outcomes to the interactionalist perspective of Tinto's theory give rise to the need for possible explanations.

One explanation pertains to the possible misspecification of the construct of academic integration by Tinto in his 1975 theoretical statements (Braxton and Lien, 2000). Tinto (1975) draws a parallel between the process of student departure from college and Durkheim's explanation (1951) for suicide. Durkheim argues that suicide takes place when an individual is not well integrated into the communities of a society. Integration into such communities assumes two forms: normative integration or similarity in beliefs and values, and a collective affiliation with other members of society. Braxton and Lien (2000) argue that if extended to departure from colleges and universities, students depart from a college or university if they fail to experience academic normative congruence or if they feel intellectually isolated from the academic communities of their college or university.

Tinto's formulations around the meaning of academic integration appear not to match the extensions of normative congruence and collective affiliation to the academic system or communities of a college or university. Specifically, Tinto's view that the normative aspect of academic integration manifests itself in the extent of personal intellectual development experienced by the student falters in its correspondence to Durkheim's notion of normative congruence as a similarity in attitudes and values. Likewise, Tinto's formulations centered on academic integration also fail to delineate the role of intellectual isolation or a sense of collective affiliation a student experiences with his or her interactions with the academic aspects of a college or university.

Another possible explanation emanates from criticisms of Tinto's theory made by Attinasi (1989, 1992). His criticisms center on the manner in which Tinto generated his theory. Tinto developed his theory from research on student departure and draws an analogy between student departure and suicide. In developing the propositions of his theory, Tinto uses Durkheim's explanation for suicide. Attinasi criticizes Tinto for drawing analogies to concepts and theories developed on other populations and phenomena. He argues that a theory of college student departure should emanate from "the sociology of everyday life" (Attinasi, 1989, p. 251). Put differently, theory on departure should develop from the direct experiences of college students. Thus, the failure of academic integration to play a role in the student departure process may stem from the manner in which Tinto developed his theory. Specifically, Attinasi argues that the analogy between normative congruence as an explanation for suicide does not adequately capture student experiences with the academic communities of their college or university.

As previously noted, Tinto's proposition that social integration positively influences subsequent institutional commitment also fails to receive strong empirical backing in four-year commuter universities. In contrast to residential colleges and universities, where this proposition garners strong empirical affirmation, commuter universities lack well-defined and well-organized social structures. Such universities generally do not have on-campus social communities or the types of students able to engage in frequent social interaction with their student peers (Tinto, 1993). This lack of well-defined and vibrant social communities provides an explanation for the failure of social integration to positively impact subsequent institutional commitment in four-year commuter universities.

Tinto's Theory: Revise or Abandon?

The validity of Tinto's theory continues as an open question in liberal arts colleges and two-year colleges and across different racial or ethnic groups. "Problematic" best describes its validity in commuter universities, but four logically interrelated propositions receive strong empirical backing in residential universities. Put differently, Tinto's theory garners partial support in this type of collegiate institution. Given the mixed pattern of support for Tinto's theory, scholars may elect to pursue two distinct paths (Braxton, 2000a). One path entails a serious revision of Tinto's theory to account for student departure in residential universities, but this path also suggests the need to abandon the application of Tinto's theory in commuter colleges and universities. The other path involves the development of new theories, one to account for student departure in four-year residential universities and the other to account for student departure in commuter institutions. We elect to pursue the first path. Accordingly, we offer a serious revision of Tinto's theory to account for student departure from residential colleges and universities in the next chapter of this volume. In a subsequent chapter, we formulate a theory to account for student departure from commuter colleges and universities.

Toward a Revision of Tinto's Theory for Residential Colleges and Universities

A S STATED IN the previous chapter, four logically interrelated propositions receive strong empirical backing in residential universities. As a consequence, a serious revision of Tinto's theory to account for student departure in residential colleges and universities appears warranted as it seems fatuous to us to "throw away" four strongly supported relationships. The revision we advance uses the four logically interrelated propositions securing strong empirical backing in residential institutions. This revision adds to these four propositions, however, by concentrating on identifying factors that influence social integration.

In this chapter, we propose a set of forces that may influence social integration and include them in a revision of Tinto's theory to account for student departure in residential colleges and universities. These forces play a major role in the revision of Tinto's theory we advance.

Influences on Social Integration

The identification of factors that influence social integration constitutes a major thrust of a revision of Tinto's interactionalist theory. We describe six influences on social integration derived from the body of literature of theory and research on college student departure. Using this body of theory and research, we derived five of these influences through a process of inductive theory construction. To elaborate, inductive theory construction begins with the findings of empirical research (Wallace, 1971). From these findings, new concepts, patterns of understandings, and generalizations emerge. In other words, a "conceptual factor analysis" of these findings occurs (Braxton, 2000b). This process parallels the open coding process used in grounded theory construction (Strauss and Corbin, 1990). These new concepts, generalizations, and understandings provide the foundation for the generation or revision of a theory. This process contributes toward a parsimonious revised theory, as it entails the delineation of underlying concepts from research findings.

Braxton and Hirschy (forthcoming) applied the process of inductive theory construction to empirical tests focusing on factors that influence social integration. They reviewed sixty-two empirical tests that identify factors that influence social integration in a statistically significant manner. The tests were conducted using traditional-age students in residential and commuter institutions. From this process, Braxton and Hirschy generated three factors that influence social integration: *commitment of the institution to student welfare, institutional integrity,* and *communal potential.*

We also engaged in this process of "conceptual factor analysis" of studies that center on the identification of factors that foster or impede social integration in residential institutions. From this process, we produced two additional concepts: *proactive social adjustment* and *psychosocial engagement.*

Ability to pay constitutes the sixth influence on social integration we include in the revision of Tinto's interactionalist theory. Cabrera, Stampen, and Hansen (1990) identify this construct and test its influence on college student departure.

The revision of Tinto's interactionalist theory proposed in this volume includes these six factors that influence social integration and the four logically related, strongly supported propositions of his theory. We describe each of these six influences on social integration in the subsections that follow.

Commitment of the Institution to Student Welfare

This construct manifests itself as an institution's abiding concern for the growth and development of its students. An institution committed to the welfare of its students also clearly communicates the high value it places on students in groups as well as individuals. The equal treatment of students and respect for them as individuals constitute additional aspects of this construct, which resonates with Tinto's first principle of effective retention. The following proposition includes this construct: *The more a student perceives that the institution is committed to the welfare of its students, the greater the student's level of social integration.*

Braxton and Hirschy (forthcoming) identify the research findings that give rise to aspects of this construct. The valuing of students, respect for students as individuals, and equal treatment of students spring from findings that suggest that fairly administering policies and rules (Berger and Braxton, 1998), communicating institutional policies and requirements (Berger and Braxton, 1998), and providing students with an opportunity to participate in the decision-making process about institutional rules and policies (Berger and Braxton, 1998) positively impact their social integration. The institution's concern for student success and adjustment arises from the positive effects of participation in a two-day student orientation program for first-year students (Pascarella, Terenzini, and Wolfle, 1986). Concern for student learning flows from the positive effects on social integration of such faculty teaching practices as active learning (Braxton, Milem, and Sullivan, 2000) and teaching skills of organization, preparation, and clarity (Braxton, Bray, and Berger, 2000).

Communal Potential

Braxton and Hirschy (forthcoming) describe *communal potential* as the extent to which a student believes that a subgroup of students exists within the college community with which that student shares similar values, beliefs, and goals. Thus, communal potential connotes the anticipation of membership in a particular community of a college or university. Community memberships emerge from residence halls (Berger, 1997), the classroom (Tinto, 1997, 2000), and student peer groups (Newcomb, 1966). The following proposition obtains: *The more a student perceives the potential of community on campus, the greater the student's level of social integration.* Put differently, the more a student perceives that he or she is likely to find a compatible social community on campus, the greater the student's level of social integration.

This construct emanates from three sets of research findings (Braxton and Hirschy, forthcoming). Berger (1997) reports that three aspects of community—identity, solidarity, and interaction—in the residence hall wield a positive effect on student social integration. The social approach and social avoidance behaviors students employ to cope with stress also affect social integration (Eaton and Bean, 1995). Specifically, formal and informal social approach behaviors foster social integration, while social avoidance behaviors impede the social integration of students who engage in such behaviors. In addition, students who receive social support from their college student peers also experience a sense of social integration (Berger and Milem, 1999; Milem and Berger, 1997).

Institutional Integrity

Institutional integrity is defined as the extent to which a college or university is true to its espoused mission and goals (Braxton and Hirschy, forthcoming). Institutional integrity demonstrates itself when the actions of a college or university's administrators, faculty, and staff are compatible with the mission and goals proclaimed by a given college or university. The following proposition springs forth: *The more a student perceives that the institution exhibits institutional integrity, the greater the student's level of social integration.*

Braxton and Hirschy (forthcoming) use two research findings to delineate this construct. Institutional integrity finds expression in institutional policies and rules that are administered in a fair manner. Berger and Braxton (1998) found that fairness in the administration of institutional policies and rules influences student social integration in a positive way. Institutional integrity also manifests itself in the extent to which student expectations for college receive fulfillment. Students who experience the fulfillment of their expectations for college also experience social integration (Helland, Stallings, and Braxton, 2001–2002). The fulfillment of expectations for college stems to some extent from admissions publications and information that accurately portrays the institution to prospective students.

Proactive Social Adjustment

This construct refers to a student's tendency to adjust in a proactive manner to the demands and pressures of social interaction in a college or university. Such a student recognizes his or her need for social affiliation and is prepared to meet the social challenges typically encountered by students in their first year of attendance. Such a student also engages in anticipatory socialization behaviors by learning the norms, attitudes, values, and behaviors required to gain membership in the social communities at her or his chosen college or university. When faced with stressful social situations, a student who makes proactive social adjustments responds to such situations by viewing this situation in a positive way. We offer the following proposition: *The greater a student's use of proactive social adjustment strategies, the greater the student's level of social integration.*

We produced this construct from several research findings. Specifically, psychological maturity wields a positive influence on student social integration (Miller, 1994). Heath (1980) holds that maturity enables individuals to adapt by "creating an optimal relation between adjusting to the demands of one's environment and fulfilling one's own needs and exercising one's fullest ranges of talents" (p. 396). Hence, increasing levels of psychological maturity better enable students to meet the social challenges typically encountered by first-year students.

This construct also stems from the finding that the need for social affiliation promotes the social integration of students (Pascarella and Chapman, 1983). Likewise, the need for communalism, a trait similar to social affiliation needs, facilitates the social integration of African American students in a predominantly white residential university (Thompson and Fretz, 1991).

Anticipatory socialization is the process by which nonmembers seek to emulate the attitudes, values, and behaviors of the group to which they seek membership (Merton, 1968). The finding that attending a two-day orientation program for first-year students positively affects the social integration of students provides some support for the role of anticipatory socialization as a proactive social adjustment strategy (Pascarella, Terenzini, and Wolfle, 1986). Such orientation programs enable students to learn the behaviors, values, and attitudes needed to establish membership in the campus community.

The strategies students employ to cope with stress also facilitate and hinder social integration and provide a basis for the construct of proactive social adjustment. To elaborate, denial as a coping strategy negatively affects social integration (Bray, Braxton, and Sullivan, 1999), whereas positive reinterpretation and growth wield a positive influence on student social integration in a residential university. Denial as a coping strategy is the individual's refusal to accept the reality of the existence of the source of stress (Carver, Scheier, and Weintraub, 1989). In contrast, efforts to see the source of stress in a positive way is the coping strategy termed "positive reinterpretation and growth" (Carver, Scheier, and Weintraub, 1989).

Psychosocial Engagement

Making new friends and getting involved in the social life of a college or university require both time and a considerable investment of psychological energy. Put differently, it requires considerable student engagement. The investment of psychological energy in interactions with peers and participation in extracurricular activities provide students with the social experiences they need to make judgments about their level of social integration. Students who have positive experiences are more likely to perceive that they are socially integrated. In contrast, students who have invested little or no psychological energy are likely to perceive that they are not well integrated into the social communities of their college or university. These formulations give rise to the following proposition: *The greater the level of psychological energy a student invests in various social interactions at his or her college or university, the greater the student's degree of social integration.*

We developed this construct from several research findings. Its primary foundation, however, rests on the notions of Astin's theory of involvement. The formulations of Astin's theory are simple: "student involvement refers to the amount of physical and psychological energy a student devotes to the academic experience" (Astin, 1984, p. 297). Research supports the role of involvement in fostering and hindering social integration. Specifically, students who participate in college social activities such as dating and participating in fraternity and sorority social activities during the spring also tend to experience greater levels of social integration (Milem and Berger, 1997). Moreover, students who exhibit no academic involvement (for example, miss classes, fail to complete coursework on time) during the spring semester display lower levels of social integration (Berger and Milem, 1999; Milem and Berger, 1997). Put differently, noninvolvement hinders social integration. Participation in extracurricular activities also fosters student social integration in a residential university (Christie and Dinham, 1991). Christie and Dinham report that students view extracurricular activities as a means to link themselves with the college environment. Opportunities to meet peers and develop friendship also emerge from such activities (Christie and Dinham, 1991).

This construct also springs from the finding that approach and avoidance behaviors used by individuals to cope with stress also influence student social integration. Informal and formal social approach behaviors positively affect social integration (Eaton and Bean, 1995). In contrast, social avoidance behaviors exert a negative influence on student social integration (Eaton and Bean, 1995). Approach behaviors are active coping behaviors, whereas avoidance behaviors permit the individual to avoid the stressful situation (Eaton and Bean, 1995). Social approach formal and informal behaviors positively impact social integration, whereas social avoidance behaviors negatively affect social integration. Informal social approach behaviors pertain to student social choices and interactions (for example, attending informal parties with friends), whereas formal social approach behaviors refer to a student's level of participation in campus leadership and the formal social structure (for example, holding office in a campus organization). Social avoidance involves behaviors that take a student away from campus such as going home for the weekend. Social approach behaviors require the investment of psychological energy, whereas social avoidance behaviors require minimal degrees of such energy.

Ability to Pay

Cabrera, Stampen, and Hansen (1990) assert that the ability to pay tempers students' adjustment to the college environment. The ability to pay eliminates or attenuates financial concerns and barriers to student participation in the social communities of their college or university (Cabrera, Stampen, and Hansen, 1990). Cabrera, Stampen, and Hansen (1990) view satisfaction with the costs of attending their chosen college or university as an ability to pay. They found that students who express satisfaction with the costs of attending their institution are more likely to persist than are students dissatisfied with the costs of attendance. Public four-year institutions served as the setting for this study by Cabrera, Stampen, and Hansen (1990). Although these scholars do not indicate whether these institutions are residential or commuter, it seems reasonable to expect that ability to pay would play a role in residential colleges and universities. The following proposition results: *The greater the level of a student's satisfaction with the costs of attending her or his chosen college or university, the greater the student's degree of social integration.*

Underlying Conceptual Orientation of the Six Influences

Economic, organizational, psychological, and sociological conceptual orientations toward student departure underlie one or more of the above influences on social integration. (The crux of these orientations was described in the first chapter of this volume.) We classify each influence according to these conceptual orientations.

Economic

Ability to pay reflects an economic perspective on student departure. Ability to pay constitutes a factor in the weighing of the costs and benefits of remaining in college, as costs of attendance decrease with an increase in the ability to pay. Weighing of costs and benefits is fundamental to an economic orientation toward student departure (St. John, Cabrera, Nora, and Asker, 2000; Tinto, 1986).

Organizational

The organizational perspective on student departure manifests itself in two of the six influences on social integration: commitment of the institution to student welfare and institutional integrity. The organizational perspective focuses on the influence of organizational structure and organizational behavior on student departure decisions (Berger and Braxton, 1998; Tinto, 1986). Organizational behavior includes the actions of administrators, faculty, and staff (Tinto, 1986). Because the actions of administrators, faculty, and staff shape both the integrity of an institution and the institution's commitment to the welfare of its students, we view these influences as reflective of an organizational perspective on student departure.

Psychological

The influence of individual psychological characteristics and psychological processes on student departure decisions characterizes a psychological conceptual orientation to this phenomena (Tinto, 1986). The crux of this perspective is that psychological processes and characteristics distinguish between students who remain enrolled from those students who decide to depart a particular college or university. Proactive social adjustment and psychosocial engagement constitute psychological entities that are posited to play an indirect role in student departure by influencing student social integration.

We view proactive social adjustment as psychological because this construct involves the ways students adjust to the demands and pressures of collegiate social interaction in a proactive rather than a reactive way. Moreover, we classify psychosocial engagement as psychological because this construct pertains to the psychological energy students expend in becoming involved in the social life of their college and in meeting and making new friends.

Sociological

A sociological orientation toward student departure emphasizes the role of social structure and social forces in the decision to depart a given college or university (Tinto, 1986). As indicated previously in this chapter, communal potential pertains to students' appraisal of their likelihood of finding a social affinity group within the social communities of their college or university. Such an appraisal results from a student's interactions with the structure of the social communities of his or her college or university.

Tinto's Theory Revisited in Residential Colleges and Universities

Our revision includes the four strongly supported and logically connected propositions of Tinto's 1975 theoretical statement (Propositions 1, 9, 10, and 13) and the six antecedents of social integration described above. We graphically portray our revision of Tinto's theory in Figure 5. Put in narrative form,

FIGURE 5
Tinto's Theory Revised for Student Departure in Residential Colleges and Universities

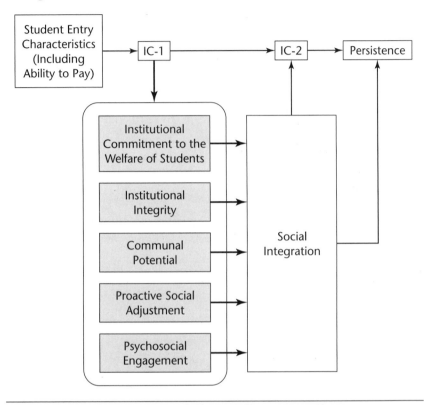

Note: Shaded boxes indicate new constructs; bold arrows indicate new propositions.
SOURCE: Adapted from Braxton, Sullivan, and Johnson, 1997; Braxton and Hirschy, forthcoming.

this revised theory is as follows: Students enter college with various characteristics. Among these entry characteristics is the ability to pay. These various student entry characteristics influence their initial level of commitment to the college or university that they chose to attend (Proposition 1). This initial level of institutional commitment shapes their perceptions of the institution's commitment to the welfare of its students, the integrity of the institution, and the potential for social community at the chosen institution. The higher the initial level of commitment to the institution, the more favorable the student's perceptions of these institutional dimensions. The student's initial commitment to the institution also influences his or her use of proactive social adjustment strategies and his or her level of psychosocial engagement. The higher the student's initial commitment to the institution, the greater his or her level of psychosocial engagement and the likelihood of his or her use of proactive social adjustment strategies.

Going to college provides students with numerous opportunities for interaction with the social dimensions of a college or university. These interactions frequently require social adjustments (Chickering and Reiser, 1993). Meeting new people and making friends constitute a set of social adjustments that create social uncertainty in many students. Such social interactions require adjustment and the investment of psychological energy. Students who use proactive rather than reactive social adjustment strategies, and students who invest considerable psychological energy into social interactions with their peers grow in their level of social confidence and certainty. Moreover, students who perceive that they are likely to find a compatible social community on campus also experience greater levels of confidence and certainty in their social interactions. Satisfaction with the costs of attending college also bolsters a student's sense of confidence and certainty.

Such students develop a strong sense of personal self-efficacy. Self-efficacy pertains to individuals' belief that they possess the ability to engage in actions necessary to achieve a particular outcome (Bandura, 1986, 1997). Because of their high levels of self-efficacy, such students feel confident in their ability to survive and adjust to the social communities of their college or university (Bean and Eaton, 2000). The ability to survive and adapt leads to social integration. Thus, the greater a student's use of proactive social adjustment strategies, the greater the student's level of social integration. Likewise, the greater the level of psychological energy a student invests in various social interactions at his or her college or university, the greater the student's degree of social integration. And the more students perceive that they are likely to find a compatible social community on campus, the greater their level of social integration. The ability to pay for college also positively influences social integration.

Students also interact with the organizational structures and agents of their college or university. The decisions and actions of administrators, faculty, and staff also impact students. Such actions and interactions help shape students' perceptions of the commitment of their institution to student welfare as well as their perceptions of the level of integrity exhibited by their institution. A sense of confidence in their college or university as an organization follows from favorable perceptions on these organizational characteristics (Bean and Eaton, 2000). Such institutional confidence leads to a sense of personal efficacy to survive and acclimate to the institution. The sense of one's ability to survive and adjust to the institution as an organization leads to social integration. Thus, the more a student perceives that the institution is committed to the welfare of its students, the greater the student's level of social integration. Moreover, the more a student perceives that the institution exhibits institutional integrity, the greater the student's level of social integration.

Social integration, in turn, affects subsequent institutional commitment. The greater the level of social integration, the greater students' subsequent commitment to the institution (Proposition 9). Likewise, students' initial level of institutional commitment affects their subsequent commitment to the institution (Proposition 10). The greater the degree of subsequent commitment to the institution, the greater the likelihood students will persist in college (Proposition 13).

Implications for Racial or Ethnic Minority Students

Because this revised theory applies to residential colleges and universities, it is a theory of student departure of the middle range. The formulations of this revised theory, however, need discussion focused on their relevance to students from various racial and ethnic groups such as African Americans, Latinos, Asian Americans, and Native Americans. Specifically, ability to pay and communal potential present possible barriers to the social integration of minority students in residential universities.

For African Americans, Latinos, and Native Americans, the ability to pay for college constitutes "first-order concerns" (Cibik and Chambers, 1991). As a consequence, minority students demonstrate a sensitivity to the costs of attending college (St. John, 1991; St. John and Noell, 1989; St. John and Starkey, 1995). Hence, minority students who perceive less of an ability to pay for college may also fail to experience a sense of social integration. Their lower degree of social integration, in turn, leads to a lesser commitment to the institution. The lower their degree of subsequent commitment to the institution, the greater the likelihood of their departure.

Like ability to pay, communal potential also has implications for minority student departure from a residential college or university. As previously indicated, communal potential refers to the anticipation of membership in a particular community of a college or university. Anticipation of membership stems from the perception that a subgroup of students exists within the college community with which the student shares similar values, beliefs, and goals. Tinto (1993) asserts that multiple social communities exist within a given college or university. Distinctive cultures characterize each of these communities. Nevertheless, some of these communities hold a peripheral position in the social structure of the institution, whereas other communities hold a position of dominance as their cultures define the character of the institution (Tinto, 1993, p. 121). These formulations receive reinforcement from Kuh and Love's perspective (2000) that students whose culture of origin is distinctly different from the dominant culture of a college or university must join one or more enclaves to experience social integration.

For minority students whose cultures of origin do not resemble the dominant culture of the social communities of their college or university, a cultural enclave or affinity group of students who share the same culture must be found. If not, such minority students will not perceive that potential for community exists for them. Minority students in residential colleges and universities with small numbers of minority students enrolled may perceive that the potential for community does not exist at their institution because few, if any, cultural enclaves or affinity student subgroups exist. Thus, such students experience less social integration because of the lack of communal potential at their chosen institution.

This chapter postulates a major revision of Tinto's interactionalist theory to explain student departure in residential colleges and universities. Because Tinto's theory lacks explanatory power in commuter institutions, the next chapter of this volume concentrates on accounting for student departure from this type of collegiate institution.

Student Departure in Commuter Colleges and Universities

IN CONTRAST TO residential institutions, commuter colleges and universities lack well-defined and -structured social communities for students to establish membership. Moreover, commuter students typically experience conflicts among their obligations to family, work, and college (Tinto, 1993). These important distinctions between residential and commuter colleges and universities indicate a need for a theory to account for student departure in commuter colleges and universities. The characteristics of commuter institutions also indicate that student departure in such institutions constitutes an ill-structured problem, a problem that Tinto's interactionalist theory fails to adequately address.

Because student departure in commuter colleges and universities presents an ill-structured problem, a theory or a conceptual model that seeks to untangle student departure in this institutional setting requires the use of constructs derived from various theoretical orientations: economic, organizational, psychological, and sociological. However, no formal economic, organizational, psychological, or sociological theory that accounts for student departure in commuter colleges and universities currently exists. Instead, scholars borrow constructs derived from these theoretical orientations to guide research on commuter colleges and universities. As a consequence, we label these orientations as conceptual rather than theoretical. In this chapter, we advance propositions using the findings of such research. These propositions provide a foundation for a theory or conceptual model of student departure in commuter colleges and universities that we propose in this chapter.

Sixteen Propositions: Elements of a Theory of Student Departure in Commuter Institutions

We organize these propositions according to their underlying conceptual orientation: economic, organizational, psychological, and sociological. Because little or no research centers on the role of organizational constructs on departure in commuter institutions, we present two propositions discussed in the previous chapter that we assert may also apply to commuter institutions. We also delineate four unclassified propositions.

We describe the findings of the research that give rise to each of these propositions, deriving these findings from studies conducted in two-year and four-year commuter institutions. Students who attend two-year colleges frequently intend to transfer to a four-year college (Tinto, 1993) or enroll for a specific course. For such students, the departure process may differ from the process for students in four-year commuter colleges and universities. We regard the departure process for two-year students enrolled in degree programs and students in four-year commuter institutions similar enough, however, to use findings from both types of commuter institutions to generate these propositions. Nevertheless, as indicated in the final chapter, "Conclusions and Recommendations for Scholarship," future research testing the theory we propose should take place in two-year and four-year commuter institutions to assess its validity in these two institutional settings. Where relevant, we also use the findings of studies conducted in four-year colleges and universities where the researcher does not indicate whether the institutions are residential or commuter. We also use the findings of studies conducted using both single- and multi-institutional samples.

Economic

As discussed in the last chapter, the elements of an economic perspective on college student departure comprise reducing costs and increasing benefits of attendance (Tinto, 1986). Departure likely results if a student perceives that the costs of attending a particular college or university exceed the benefits of attendance (Braxton, 2003). Such a conceptual orientation leads to the following proposition bolstered by empirical research: *The lower the costs of college attendance incurred by students, the greater their likelihood of persisting in college.*

Financial aid serves to reduce the cost of college attendance. Research demonstrates that student financial aid facilitates student retention. Based on the results of a meta-analysis of studies on the direct influence of financial aid on college student departure, Murdock (1987) reports that the effect of financial aid on student departure is quite small but positive. Moreover, the effect of financial aid on persistence, albeit small, is greater for students in two-year colleges than in four-year colleges (Murdock, 1987). Murdock's meta-analysis compared two groups of students: those receiving some financial aid with those not receiving any financial aid. Stampen and Cabrera (1986) make a similar comparison for students enrolled in the University of Wisconsin system. Their findings lend some support to the conclusions advanced by Murdock (1987). Students who receive no financial aid demonstrate a greater probability of departure than students who receive some type of financial aid. Moreover, Schuh (1999) found that the total amount of financial aid received wields a positive influence on college student retention.

The type of financial aid received also influences college student retention. Grants, loans, and work-study each positively impact student persistence (Cofer and Somers, 1999; St. John, Kirschstein, and Noell, 1991; Voorhees, 1985).

In contrast, increases in the cost of attending college reduce the likelihood of student persistence. Specifically, the greater the net price and net costs of attendance, the more likely student departure occurs (St. John and Starkey, 1995). Likewise, additional costs associated with attending college such as housing, food, and travel expenses tend to decrease the likelihood of student persistence (St. John, Paulsen, and Starkey, 1996).

Organizational

In the previous chapter, we classified commitment of the institution to student welfare and institutional integrity as reflective of the organizational conceptual orientation to student departure. Although these two constructs spring from research conducted in residential collegiate institutions, these two organizational constructs may also influence student decisions to depart from a commuter college or university. Accordingly, we extend these two constructs to the case of the commuter college or university by presenting the following two propositions: *The more a student perceives that the institution is committed to the welfare of its students, the lower the likelihood of the student's departure. The more a student perceives that the institution exhibits institutional integrity, the lower the likelihood of the student's departure.*

Psychological

As discussed in the last chapter, the role of psychological characteristics and psychological processes in the departure of college students characterizes the psychological orientation to understanding this phenomenon (Tinto, 1986, 1993). We present the following five propositions that involve psychological processes or personality traits in the departure decisions of students enrolled in commuter collegiate institutions:

Motivation to graduate from college exerts a positive influence on student persistence. Motivation to make steady progress toward college completion also positively impacts student retention. Motivation manifests itself in such ways as the importance to oneself of completing college (Hagedorn, Maxwell, and Hampton, 2001–2002) and the purpose of attending college (Voorhees, 1987). The importance to oneself of completing college affects student persistence through the second and third semesters of attendance but not the first semester (Hagedorn, Maxwell, and Hampton, 2001–2002). Likewise, transfer to another two-year college for the purpose of college attendance positively impacts persistence (Voorhees, 1987).

The greater a student's need for control and order in his or her daily life, the greater the student's likelihood of departure. This proposition is derived from findings related to the role of two personality traits in the student departure process at commuter institutions: locus of control and judging. Locus of control exerts a direct influence on student persistence, as students who attribute events or outcomes to their own efforts are more likely to depart than are student who attribute events to luck or fate (Bers, 1985). Put differently, students with an internal locus of control are more likely to depart than students who hold an external locus of control. Judging, a trait similar to an internal locus of control, also exerts a negative influence on the retention of students (Zhang and RiCharde, 1998). Judging reflects an individual's inclination to control the world through deliberate and planned decision making in contrast to a more flexible orientation. Judging also reflects an orientation more toward closure than process (Zhang and RiCharde, 1998).

The stronger a person's belief that he or she can achieve a desired outcome through his or her own efforts, the less likely the student will depart from college. This proposition stems from self-efficacy theory. Self-efficacy pertains to an individual's belief that he or she has the ability to engage in actions necessary to attain a particular outcome (Bandura, 1986, 1997). Bean and Eaton (2000) delineate self-efficacy as a possible influence on student departure. Research tends to show that self-efficacy exerts a positive influence on student persistence (Zhang and RiCharde, 1998).

The greater a student's awareness of the effects of his or her decisions and actions on other people, the greater the student's likelihood of departure from college. Erwin (1983) postulates four stages of increasing intellectual sophistication. Empathy, one of the four stages, tends to negatively impact student persistence (Zhang and RiCharde, 1998). In other words, students who exhibit an awareness of the effects of their decisions and actions on others are more likely to depart from college.

The greater a student's need for affiliation, the greater the student's likelihood of departure from college. Stern (1970) indicates that the need for affiliation reflects the extent to which an individual is friendly, likes to participate in activities with others, and holds a group orientation. Research tends to indicate that affiliation needs directly and negatively affect student persistence in nonresidential institutional settings (Pascarella and Chapman, 1983).

Sociological

We indicated in the previous chapter that the sociological perspective stresses the influence of social structure and social forces on college student departure (Tinto, 1986). The status attainment process provides one basis for identifying constructs that have sociological conceptual underpinnings. Status attainment pertains to the social processes that influence how individuals achieve positions of status in society. College attendance (Hossler, Braxton, and Coopersmith, 1989) and persistence in college (Tinto, 1986) are two key aspects of the status attainment process. Family socioeconomic status and the influence of significant others constitute important social forces posited to play a role in the status attainment process (Alwin and Otto, 1977; Sewell, Haller, and Portes, 1969; Sewell and Hauser, 1975; Sewell and Shah, 1978). Other social forces that may affect student retention include the classroom as a community and mechanisms of anticipatory socialization. We delineate the following four propositions that entail such social forces:

As parents' educational level increases, the likelihood of student departure from a commuter college or university also increases. Parents' educational level provides an index of family socioeconomic status. Halpin (1990) found that the educational level of the father negatively impacts student persistence. In other words, students whose fathers have higher levels of education are more likely to depart a commuter college. Hagedorn, Maxwell, and Hampton (2001–2002) found a similar pattern for a combined measure of the educational level of the mother and the father. Specifically, parents' educational level negatively affects student persistence through the first and second semesters of attendance. Under the campus environment dimension of our proposed theory of student departure in commuter colleges and universities, we offer an explanation for this counterintuitive proposition.

Support from significant others for college attendance decreases the likelihood of student departure from a commuter college or university. Parents, high school friends, and teachers are significant others. Research tends to indicate that support or encouragement for going to college from such individuals significant to the student tends to increase their prospects of persisting in college (Cabrera and others, 1999; Mutter, 1992; Okun, Benin, and Brandt-Williams, 1996; Pike, Schroeder, and Berry, 1997; Schwartz, 1990). Moreover, Cabrera and others (1999) note that support from significant others impacts the persistence of both white and African American students in a positive manner.

The probability of student departure from a commuter college or university decreases for students who participate in communities of learning. Tinto (1997, 2000) posits that college classrooms constitute one form of a community of learning where academic and social systems of a college or university intersect. Participation in the community of the classroom affords an entry point for students, especially new students, for further involvement in the academic and social systems of their college or university. Learning communities take shape through block scheduling of courses so that the same group of students takes a set of courses together (Tinto, 1997, 1998, 2000). Research tends to suggest that participation in a learning community positively influences student persistence in college (Tinto, 1997).

The probability of student departure from a commuter college or university increases for students who engage in anticipatory socialization before entering college. Anticipatory socialization is the process by which nonmembers seek to emulate the attitudes, values, and behaviors of the group in which they seek membership (Merton, 1968). Getting ready behaviors constitute a mechanism of anticipatory socialization. Nora, Attinasi, and Matonak (1990) identify early expectations for college and prematriculation experiences as forms of getting ready behaviors. Such getting ready behaviors wield a direct but negative influence on student persistence in commuter collegiate institutions (Nora, Attinasi, and Matonak, 1990). We provide an explanation for this counterintuitive proposition under the campus environment dimension of our proposed theory of student departure in commuter colleges and universities.

Additional Propositions

We identify four additional propositions. The first two propositions posit relationships between student entry characteristics and initial and subsequent institutional commitment. As discussed in the chapter "Tinto's Interactionalist Theory," tests of these two propositions garner strong empirical affirmation in commuter institutions (Braxton, Sullivan, and Johnson, 1997). Although Tinto's theory includes these propositions, they are not core propositions to the interactionalist perspective espoused by his theory. These propositions take the following form:

Student entry characteristics affect the level of initial commitment to the institution. The initial level of institutional commitment to the institution affects the subsequent level of commitment to the institution.

The third proposition pertains to a link between academic integration and subsequent institutional commitment not specified by Tinto's theory (1975).

As indicated in the chapter "Tinto's Interactionalist Theory," Braxton and Lien (2000) suggest the possibility of such a relationship. They report that seven out of ten tests of this relationship affirm it in commuter institutions. Accordingly, we advance the following proposition:

The greater the degree of academic integration perceived by students, the greater their degree of subsequent commitment to the institution.

The fourth proposition originates from Tinto's interactionalist theory (1975). This proposition, however, is not core to the interactionalist perspective that underlies Tinto's theory. As indicated in "Tinto's Interactionalist Theory," Tinto (1993) strongly asserts that his theory is not a systems theory and that tests conducted using multi-institutional samples violate the underlying interactionalist assumptions of this theory. To be true to such underlying assumptions, we did not present it as evidence of validity for Tinto's perspective for commuter colleges and universities as support, because this proposition emerges from multi-institutional tests. We present it herein, however, not as a proposition of Tinto's theory but as an element toward the generation of a theory that accounts for student departure in commuter colleges and universities. Braxton, Sullivan, and Johnson (1997) report support for this proposition in multi-institutional samples of commuter institutions. This proposition is as follows:

The greater the degree of subsequent commitment to the institution, the greater the likelihood of student persistence in college.

Formulating a Theory of Student Departure in Commuter Colleges and Universities

These sixteen propositions provide the basis for the development of theory to account for student departure from commuter colleges and universities. Figure 6 displays this theory in graphic form. The theory takes the following form.

The basic elements of this theory include student entry characteristics, the external environment, the campus environment, and the academic

FIGURE 6
Theory of Student Departure in Commuter Colleges and Universities

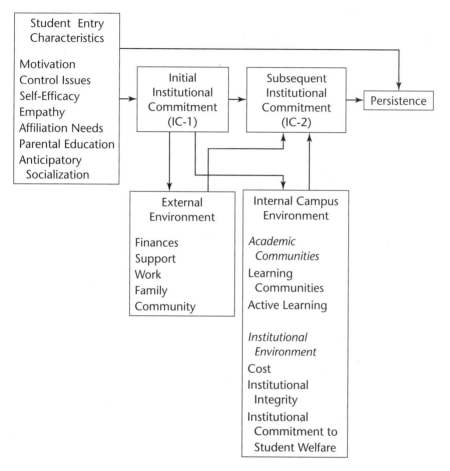

communities of the institution. These various elements directly influence either subsequent commitment to the institution or the departure decisions of students enrolled in commuter colleges and universities.

Student Entry Characteristics
Characteristics with which students enter commuter colleges and universities play a significant role in the student departure process in this type of collegiate institution. Some entry characteristics (for example, family background,

academic ability, and high school academic achievement) affect the initial level of commitment that a student holds for his or her chosen college or university. This initial level of commitment also influences the student's level of commitment to the institution that develops as a result of attending the chosen institution. This subsequent level of commitment to the institution, in turn, affects student departure decisions. Specifically, the greater the level of subsequent commitment to the institution, the greater the likelihood of student persistence.

External Environment

Student entry characteristics also affect student adjustments to both the external environment and the environment of the commuter institution. To elaborate, a wide range of students attend commuter colleges and universities. First-time first-year students living at home with their parents, unmarried students who work and attend college, and students with families who work and attend college represent some the categories that typify commuter students (Stewart and Rue, 1983). These students may attend part time as well as full time. Students in the traditional college-going age group of 18 to 21 years old as well as adult students attend commuter colleges and universities (Bean and Metzner, 1985).

Commuter students frequently have obligations distinct from attending college. For some, these obligations include work and family (Tinto, 1993). Thus, external forces such as family, work, and community greatly define their day-to-day activities (Webb, 1990). As a consequence, such external forces play an important role in the departure decisions of students attending commuter collegiate institutions. The time commitments of work and attending college may negatively affect the families of commuter students. Departure from college may result for those students aware of the negative effects of their college attendance on such significant others. Put differently, students with the personality trait of empathy tend to be more likely to depart from commuter colleges and universities. Consequently, encouragement and support for attending college become important. Students who receive support and encouragement to attend college from significant others are less likely to depart. The negative effects on family life because of work and attending college lessen if the financial costs of attending college are minimized. Likewise, support and encouragement to attend college from significant others increase if the financial costs of attending college are minimized. Thus, the lower the costs of college attendance incurred by students, the greater their likelihood of persisting in college.

Campus Environment

The characteristics of the students attending a particular college or university play a substantial part in the shaping of its environments (Clark, 1972; Holland, 1997; Pascarella and Terenzini, 1991). The environments of commuter colleges and universities are no exception. The characteristics of students who commute to college mold to a large extent the environments of such collegiate institutions. These characteristics also affect the adjustment of students to the institutional environment of the commuter college or university.

Commuter students spend a very limited amount of time on the campus of a commuter college or university (Tinto, 1993). The time spent on campus typically entails attending class and meeting degree requirements (Tinto, 1993). Students hurry to meet their classes and hurry to leave the campus to go to work or to go home. Thus, many students come and go throughout the day. In urban settings, buses, trains, and cars come and go from the campus. All forms of comings and goings create a "buzzing confusion." The order that exists comes from the daily schedule of classes meeting at their appointed times.

Commuter students' time on campus focuses primarily on classes, often at the exclusion of other campus involvement. Students who have significant commitments off campus, such as work and family, have other places where they need to spend their time. Thus, the hurried nature of their campus experiences reflects well-worn paths between the parking lot and the classrooms. Without meaningful interactions with other students, commuters feel isolated and disconnected, feelings that contribute to a perception of chaos and confusion.

Student adjustment to the confusion of the ambience of the commuter institution requires certain personality traits. Motivation to make steady progress toward graduation and to graduate from college is a necessary personality trait. Hence, motivation to graduate from college exerts a positive influence on student persistence. Motivation to make steady progress toward college completion also positively impacts student retention. Given the role of external forces and the confusion that characterizes the commuter institution, students must also believe that their efforts in attending college will result in academic success and graduation. Put differently, commuter students must have high levels of self-efficacy, another necessary personality trait. Accordingly, the stronger a person's belief that he or she can achieve a desired outcome through his or her own efforts, the less likely he or she will depart from a commuter college or university. Moreover, students who require order in their daily lives and need control over events in their lives may experience difficulty adjusting to the confusing nature of the commuter institution. Those students with a high need for order may be especially challenged by the need to balance academic work with the demands of family and work. Consequently, the greater a student's need for control and order in his or her daily life, the greater his or her likelihood of departure.

The lack of well-defined and -structured social communities for students to establish membership also characterizes the campus environments of commuter colleges and universities. The failure of social communities to form results from the characteristics of the students who attend commuter institutions and from the confusing nature of the campus environment. For some students, the lack of social communities leads to their departure. Specifically, the role of the need for social affiliation, parental educational levels, and anticipatory socialization activities in the student departure process result from the lack of definitive social communities. Students with a need for social affiliation find the lack of social communities problematic. Thus, the greater a student's need for social affiliation, the more likely he or she is to depart from a commuter college or university.

Parental educational level also influences student departure because of the lack of social community at commuter institutions. The images students hold of the characteristics colleges and universities should possess come from a variety of sources such as parents, teachers, high school college counselors, students, movies, television, and the media. "Residentiality" represents one element of the image of a college or university (Kamens, 1977). Kamens views residentiality as physical and social isolation from the student's life before attending college. Laden, Milem, and Crowson (2000) suggest that residentiality may account for varying rates of departure by institutional type. The ill-defined structure of the social communities of the commuter institution sharply contrasts with this notion of "residentiality." Parents who attended college are more likely to hold residentiality as an important characteristic of a college or university. As a consequence, as parental educational level increases, the likelihood of departure from a commuter college or university increases. Students who engage in anticipatory socialization behaviors also more likely depart because they learn from such behaviors that commuter colleges and universities do not fully resemble the images they hold of colleges and universities. Put differently, students who engage in "getting ready behaviors" such as forming early expectations for college and participating in prematriculation activities (Nora, Attinasi, and Matonak, 1990) learn that "residentiality" does not accurately depict day-to-day enrollment at a commuter institution.

Although student characteristics play a significant role in shaping the campus environment, characteristics of the commuter college or university as an organization also play an important part in the student departure process. In particular, two organizational characteristics directly affect subsequent levels of a student's commitment to his or her institution. These two characteristics also wield an indirect influence on student departure decisions.

These organizational characteristics are *commitment of the institution to the welfare of its students* and *institutional integrity.* Every commuter college or university exhibits these characteristics in varying degrees, from little or no presence of the characteristic to its being an important and defining characteristic of the organization.

These two characteristics manifest themselves in the actions of administrators, faculty, and staff of the commuter college or university. Students who perceive through the actions of these organizational agents that commitment to the welfare of students represents an abiding concern of their college or university develop a stronger subsequent level of commitment to their institution. The greater the degree of subsequent commitment to the institution, the greater the likelihood of student persistence in college.

The actions of administrators, faculty, and staff also provide students with an opportunity to assess the extent to which their institution remains true to its mission and goals. Greater levels of subsequent institutional commitment develop in students who perceive that their college or university exhibits such institutional integrity. The greater the degree of subsequent commitment to the institution, the greater the likelihood of student persistence in college.

Academic Communities

As a consequence of the absence of well-defined social structures in commuter colleges and universities, the academic dimensions of the commuter institution play a consequential role in the student departure process. Students' perceptions of their degree of integration into the academic spheres of a commuter college or university shape their level of subsequent commitment to their chosen institution. The greater the level of academic integration perceived by students, the greater their level of subsequent commitment to the institution. The greater their level of subsequent commitment to the institution, the greater their likelihood of continued enrollment.

The community of the classroom represents another aspect of the academic dimension of commuter colleges and universities that directly influences student departure decisions. Small communities develop around the college classroom, a community for each course. Such communities develop, however, only if faculty members actively involve students in the process of learning. Active learning refers to class activities that involve students in thinking about the course subject matter (Bonwell and Eison, 1991). Such activities include cooperative learning, debates, role playing, discussion, and pair and group work. Although student learning constitutes the intended purpose of such communities, the classroom in a commuter college or university also provides limited opportunities for student social interaction. Student social interaction results from participation in active learning activities. Student friendship may develop from such interactions. Students with a high need for social affiliation may experience some satisfaction when enrolled in courses offered by faculty who engage students in active learning.

Although active learning is a basic requirement for the formation of the community of the classroom, the block scheduling of courses so that the same group of students take a set of courses together supplies the optimum form for their development (Tinto, 1997, 1998, 2000). A central theme undergirds these courses, which assume the form of a learning community.

Participation in a learning community positively influences student persistence in college (Tinto, 1997). Such participation also fosters academic integration. Moreover, students enrolled in courses offered by faculty who engage students in active learning experience greater degrees of academic integration and are also less likely to depart from college.

Implications for Racial or Ethnic Minority Students

As we mentioned earlier, student departure from commuter institutions often is more influenced by external forces that shape the character of students' lives off campus than by events that happen within the academic or social spheres of the campus (Tinto, 1993). Moreover, though the competing external pressures of families, peers, and work for racial or ethnic minority students are similar in nature to those for other students, they may well be more intense. The conflict between the obligations of family, work, and those of the college may also be greater for students from minority groups.

Racial or ethnic minority students often feel pressured to spend more time with family or to oversee family matters, which decreases the amount of time available to engage the academic and social aspects of the institution. Also, because commuter institutions lack well-defined and -structured social communities, limited opportunities exist to interact with faculty and peers outside the classroom setting in contrast to residential institutions.

Many racial or ethnic minority students who attend commuter institutions are first-generation collegians and are from low socioeconomic status backgrounds (Tinto, 1993). Because of their parents' educational experiences, the students' secondary school experiences, and their peers' educational expectations, many students do not enter commuter institutions with a strong commitment to graduate. Further, their home environment and external responsibilities are different from students who attend residential colleges and universities. Minority students who attend commuter institutions often have jobs, live away from campus, and have demanding family responsibilities (Nora, Cabrera, Hagedorn, and Pascarella, 1996). In this case, departure decisions are influenced by how students negotiate these conflicts and how much support students receive from significant others for college attendance. For those minority students whose initial goal or institutional commitments are weak, the impact of significant others can have a positive or negative influence on persistence (Tinto, 1993). When the value orientations of significant others support the goals of college attendance, they positively influence persistence (Cabrera and others, 1999; Nora, 1987). When they oppose them, the reverse may apply. To that end, one would expect that racial and ethnic minorities often face barriers while attempting to complete degree programs.

The costs of attending a commuter college or university present a particular problem for racial or ethnic minority students. Minority students who attend commuter institutions are more sensitive to costs of college tuition and less willing to use educational loans (Kaltenbaugh, St. John, and Starkey, 1999). For example, tuition costs wield a negative influence on persistence for African American students (Kaltenbaugh, St. John, and Starkey, 1999; Somers, Cofer, Below, and Freeman, 2002). These students traditionally have less money to attend college and lack pertinent information about financial aid opportunities such as federal, state, private, and college aid (Hu and St. John, 2001; Nora, 1990; Olivas, 1986). Those attending two-year colleges often do not have the assistance of high school guidance counselors, teachers, peers, and parents to help negotiate the financial realities of the college experience. Financial stress and inadequate information about financial aid and the application process negatively influence the departure decisions of Hispanic students (Solberg, 1993).

Moreover, the patterns of financing college for African Americans and Hispanics are different from those for their Caucasian counterparts. Baird (1984) found that 64 percent of Caucasian students relied on parental aid as opposed to 47 percent for African American students and 27 percent for Hispanic students. These students used federal aid (for example, grants, loans, work-study) and college aid (for example, scholarships), and they held jobs (for example, full-time and part-time employment) to pay their tuition considerably more frequently than Caucasian students. To reinforce this distinction, most Hispanic students (more than 60 percent) receive aid from only one source— Basic Educational Opportunity Grants, known as Pell grants since 1981 (Olivas, 1986).

The formulations of this theory we postulate to account for student departure in commuter colleges and universities carry implications for institutional policy and practice directed toward reducing institutional rates of student departure. Likewise, the formulations of the revision of Tinto's interactionalist theory for residential colleges and universities also hold implications for efforts to reduce institutional rates of departure. The next two chapters focus on the implications for policy and practice of the theoretical frameworks presented earlier.

Exemplary Student Retention Programs

THROUGHOUT THE decades of research conducted on college student persistence issues, both research findings and professional practice influenced the evolution of retention programs. Empirical studies that explore the nature of student departure decisions inform the praxes of how colleges and universities can more effectively help students meet their educational goals. Similarly, through the public sharing and assessment of established retention initiatives, institutional leaders can learn what has worked (and less commonly, what has not worked) in various institutional settings. The gleaned ideas can then be assessed regarding potential value for other campuses. This chapter reviews existing literature regarding retention initiatives that contribute to student persistence at colleges and universities and offers examples of nine exemplary programs.

Sources of Retention Programs

As a result of the sustained interest in understanding the student departure process, descriptions of retention programs exist in several forms. Although it is beyond the scope of this chapter to provide a comprehensive list of retention initiatives, some rich repositories are briefly described here.

The ERIC Clearinghouse for Community Colleges (2000) provides a list of annotated bibliographies of articles on retention programs in community college settings. Some of the annotated bibliographies in the ERIC Clearinghouse on Higher Education–produced *Critical Issues Bibliography (CRIB) Sheets* include student retention programs. The CRIB sheets address issues related to targeted populations, such as Hispanic (2002b), Native American (2002c), and underrepresented students in general (2002d). CRIB sheets exist also for various other retention approaches, such as summer bridge programs (2002e) and early intervention strategies (2002a). The AASCU/Sallie Mae National Retention Project focused on the institutional capacity of state colleges or universities as the unit of analysis versus student characteristics or behaviors (Arrington, 1994). Phrased differently, the project endeavored to help state institutions create organizational change to improve their effectiveness. Strategies focused on ways to provide access to and promote success of their students, particularly those from underrepresented groups. One of the outcomes of the project was *Campus Practices for Student Success: A Compendium of Model Programs* (American Association of State Colleges and Universities, 1994). This report includes descriptions of retention programs at sixty-nine state institutions.

No comprehensive list of retention programs exists, though resources abound in many academic and professional journals, such as *Journal of College Student Retention* and *The Journal of the Freshman Year Experience*. Retention is a focal point of study in several types of publications; books and monographs also offer examples of institutional retention programs (see Gaither, 1999; Hossler, 1991; Stodt and Klepper, 1987; and Tinto, 1993). College and university Internet Web sites provide additional information about their programs.

Selecting Exemplary Retention Programs

Researchers offer guidelines on how to implement and evaluate retention programs (see Dolence, 1991; Hossler, 1991; Wilcox, 1991). A keystone theme in such publications acknowledges that retention strategies, programs, and assessments must take into consideration the larger context of the individual institution, such as institutional mission, goals, and resources. Further, retention initiatives should be linked to other institutional strategies to help students achieve their educational goals. Finally, multiple factors influence student persistence decisions, so no single program will address all students' needs. Similarly, voluntary decisions to stay or leave an institution remain with individuals, so programs must consider individual needs to be effective.

According to Tinto (1993), retention programs can be assessed according to the following three principles:

1. Institutions are committed to the students they serve. The welfare of the student is primary.
2. Individuals at the institution are committed to the education of all students (not just some).
3. Individuals at the institution are committed to the development of supportive social and academic communities in which all students are integrated as full members. It is the institution's obligation (through its programs) to provide ways for students to integrate into the community (pp. 146–147).

Braxton (1999) recommends that Tinto's three principles for effective retention be used to select and evaluate programs and policies. Programs that are consistent with one or more of Tinto's principles of effective retention or are grounded in research findings offer the most promise to reduce institutional rates of departure (Braxton and Mundy, 2001–2002).

This review centers on exemplary programs. *Exemplary* in this context refers to programs that meet at least two of Tinto's three principles of effective retention. *Retention program* refers to intentional institutional actions that devote college or university resources to the aim of increasing student persistence. Institutional resources can take several forms, such as funding, personnel time, and space.

Elements of the nine exemplary programs reflect examples of the proposed constructs identified in the chapters titled "Toward a Revision of Tinto's Theory in Residential Colleges and Universities" and "Student Departure in Commuter Colleges and Universities (for example, institutional commitment to the welfare of students). Regarding the following retention program descriptions, if institutions were identified in the original source, the names are included. Occasionally, a secondary source provided the institutional identity, but the college or university was referenced in the text only by institutional type. The programs are listed alphabetically; no ranking is implied.

Nine Exemplary Retention Programs

Campus Retention Committee

The Campus Retention Committee (CRC) is a student-initiated and -run minority retention program at UCLA (Maldonado, Rhoads, and Chang, 2002). Funded by student fees, the CRC plays a coordinating function for activities designed to improve graduation rates of minority students. The CRC financially supports retention projects of five student organizations of under-represented populations: African American, American Indian, Latino, Filipino, and Vietnamese. The central component of the retention programs is peer counseling, through which most of the projects take shape. Students from each of these groups serve as peer leaders and organize seminars to promote academic success. All interested students may use CRC services.

Through a variety of methods, the CRC promotes strategic thinking about how individual and collective resources can be directed toward academic success. The CRC offers staff training and development activities, various educational programs, peer-supported study halls, and study groups. Student counselors also provide internship and mentorship programs.

Though there are differences in the five student organizations' retention projects, all share common objectives: help students acquire necessary knowledge, skills, and social connections; develop connections and commitments to community; and challenge institutional norms (p. 13). Students help each other develop academic skills and supportive relationships with others in the community. They also support the maintenance of connections with students' home communities. Further, by providing guidance for critical thinking, the student counselors assist their peers to devise strategies to meet targeted academic goals. This empowering process of maximizing group resources, identifying obstacles and opportunities, and creating an action plan provides a model for creating change in areas that extend beyond their semester grades.

The program meets Tinto's three criteria of effective programs; in addition, the CRC exemplifies several antecedents to social integration described in the chapter "Toward a Revision of Tinto's Theory for Residential Colleges and Universities." Located at a major research university, the Campus Retention

Committee retention program empowers students to positively influence their academic performance. Students who develop strategies for academic success may seek to emulate peers who have already demonstrated achievement. By learning from others' experiences, new students may experience less stress in their transition to collegiate academic demands and more support for proactive social adjustment, one of the sources of influence on social integration delineated in the chapter. Understanding what is expected of them in the college environment enables students to more easily become productive community members and connect with other students. Further, students who serve as peer counselors experience opportunities to help others succeed, investing considerable energy in their roles. This energy is an example of psychosocial engagement.

College Process Review

Student perceptions of key instructional and administrative processes were studied at a community college to determine potential changes that could have a high impact on improving student persistence (Heverly, 1999). Through this approach, changes were identified in student services and instruction to improve retention.

Two telephone surveys were conducted with a random sample of first-year students to inquire about their satisfaction with experiences they encountered with admissions, advising, course scheduling, registration, financial aid, billing, and classroom instruction. The first survey took place after the third week of fall classes and focused on student interactions from the time they applied to the college to that point. The second survey was administered after the advising period for the spring semester registration and addressed student experiences after the third week of classes.

Comparisons between the group of students who enrolled for the spring semester with those who departed indicated that those who returned were significantly more satisfied with the college processes. The inquiry focused on specific, "high-leverage" (p. 5) actions that the college could adjust to increase retention. For example, the study revealed that nonreturning students found the financial aid office less helpful than those who returned. As a result of this finding, campus leaders asked for volunteers from other campus offices to provide extra telephone support during peak times in the financial aid office. The volunteers talked with the callers, took key information, and promised that a financial aid staff member would return the call within twenty-four hours. Knowing this was a temporary solution, administrators then considered other approaches (or levers) to improve student satisfaction with encounters with the financial aid office. Similar reflections occurred regarding the other survey items that departing students found less satisfying than their peers.

This program exemplifies formative assessment of ongoing college activities that can be adjusted to increase student persistence. Such an evaluation represents Tinto's three criteria necessary for successful retention programs. By asking students about their perceptions of services offered by the institution, the college process review demonstrates an institutional commitment to the welfare of students, a construct common to the theories we advanced earlier. Students who are asked to offer suggestions of how the institution can improve can also assess the willingness of institutional leaders to sincerely listen and respond to students' concerns, an indicator of institutional integrity, another common construct.

Collegia Program

The Collegia Program (Schmitz, 2002) provides a "home away from home" in several campus locations for commuter students at Seattle University, an urban institution with approximately three-quarters of enrolled students living off campus. Rooms are equipped with computers, comfortable furniture, a kitchen, and other amenities to help commuters feel at home on campus. Three living-learning communities have been created to assist students who live off campus foster relationships outside the classroom with peers, graduate student staff, and faculty associates. One collegium remains open as a haven for summer students. The National Association of Student Personnel Administrators in 2002 selected this retention program as an exemplary program.

The Collegia (the Latin plural for "gathering place") Program meets two of Tinto's criteria for effective retention programs: the institution is committed to the students it serves and to the development of supportive and academic communities. Providing space on campus to welcome commuters while they are on campus, the institution provides a comfortable place for them to integrate into the community. By devoting physical space and personnel staffing to foster social connections among commuting students, the Collegia Program demonstrates institutional commitment to the welfare of students. This program also addresses the construct *communal potential,* though we note that this construct is not part of the theory we advance in the chapter "Student Departure in Commuter Colleges and Universities."

Continuing the Legacy of African American Success

Continuing the Legacy of African American Success (C.L.A.S.S.) is a residence life–sponsored program established to enrich the experience of African American students who live in the residence halls at a predominantly Caucasian-American research-extensive university (Taylor and Miller, 2002). Peers are selected as C.L.A.S.S. Advocates (CAs) to reside with and address the needs and concerns of African American students who live in one of six residential communities. CAs are expected to encourage students with cultural differences to interact; serve as a source of concern, support, and referral to all students, especially African Americans; and promote retention and academic success through programming and support (Department of University Housing, 2002). Though it is targeted to African American needs and concerns, all students can participate.

According to Taylor and Miller (2002), the students who participated in the C.L.A.S.S. residential communities were most distinguished from those who lived elsewhere by one factor: student leadership opportunities. The concept of leadership opportunities may have offered several avenues of psychological support, such as a sense of importance, autonomy, and interdependence. Specifically, leadership opportunities influenced African American students' levels of several psychosocial factors (such as sense of worth and competence, social integration, affiliation with ethnic others, guidance, and reliable alliances).

Through a peer network, the C.L.A.S.S. program may provide a residential haven for students of color on a predominantly white Caucasian campus. C.L.A.S.S. meets all three of Tinto's three criteria for effective programs. Also, the program includes specific objectives for peer leader involvement, promoting meaningful social interactions between students and peer leaders. As such, C.L.A.S.S exemplifies both psychosocial engagement and communal potential, two antecedents to social integration. Additionally, the institution devotes physical space to assist students in making connections with their peers, which can be considered an indicator of institutional commitment to student welfare.

Decision Tree

At a highly residential university with a relatively low attrition rate (that is, the six-year graduation rate equals 86 percent), the Psychological and Counseling Center (PCC) staff developed several strategies to identify and support students who considered leaving the institution. Among the approaches was to simply ask students directly whether they were thinking about transferring. The program was named "Decision Tree" (Sieveking and Perfetto, 2000–2001), emphasizing the various factors that influence students' reasons for staying or withdrawing.

After the first four to six weeks of school, first-year students received letters asking whether they were seriously considering withdrawing from the university, and if so, whether they would consider discussing their decision with someone. About 20 percent of the students returned the reply card. Of that group, about 20 percent responded that they were seriously considering leaving. Of those seriously considering withdrawing, about 60 percent were willing to meet with someone about their decision. The PCC staff met with those individuals and helped them better understand why they wanted to leave. Counselors then made internal referrals (for example, psychotherapy, study skills review, stress management) and external referrals (for example, to academic advisers, residence life, religious counsel, student activities, and financial aid staff) to help students.

The authors noted that the student participants in the Decision Tree program were most likely those who preferred to stay, even though they considered leaving. It is this group that might benefit most from referrals based on their individual situations. Put differently, those who had already decided to leave may not have been interested in talking with someone about that choice.

The Decision Tree program provides an example of a retention initiative coordinated by a single office that then collaborates with other offices at a private research-extensive institution. It meets all three of Tinto's criteria for successful retention programs and exemplifies two antecedents to social integration: institutional commitment to the welfare of students and institutional integrity.

Freshmen Academic Support and Tracking Program

The Fulbright College of Arts and Sciences at the University of Arkansas developed the Freshmen Academic Support and Tracking (FAST) program in 1994 to increase student retention. The aim of the program (Mangold and others, 2002–2003) was to provide experiences that would assist students' integration into the academic community, thereby improving student persistence patterns. The FAST program combines a unit scheduling program with a faculty mentor experience for first-year students. Students who participate in FAST share nine hours of classes in the fall and six hours of classes in the spring with a cohort of their peers. Additionally, a faculty member mentor meets weekly with the cohort of students in a one-credit class. Before teaching the class, mentors attended workshops that addressed social and academic transition issues students may experience. Throughout the year, faculty mentors interact with the students in a variety of settings outside the classroom, such as monthly dinners, and social and academic events. As a cohort, students participate in activities together outside the classroom.

Researchers found that students in FAST had significantly lower ACT scores, had fewer friends from their high schools, and were younger than those not in the FAST program. Even with these added risk factors, the FAST participants were more likely to persist through their first year and to graduate than those who did not participate (Mangold and others, 2002–2003).

Faculty mentoring and a class cohort experience (also known as block scheduling) are featured in the FAST program. The FAST program meets all three of Tinto's criteria of effective programs and proffers several opportunities for students to achieve social integration. Through the extended contact with other students, new students learn the attitudes, values, and behaviors of college students, which increases communal potential. The time and energy students expend in FAST exemplify another antecedent to social integration, psychosocial engagement. Spending time with faculty members to learn what is expected of college students and developing strategies to meet those expectations is an indicator of proactive social adjustment.

The Puente Project

What began with two faculty members who were concerned about the high Latino student attrition rate at a community college evolved into a state-level retention program. The Puente Project (*puente* means "bridge" in Spanish) welcomes Latino students into California state community colleges by creating bridges between the educational experience and their cultural community (Laden, 1998; McGrath and Galaviz, 1996). McGrath and Galaviz (1996) created the Puente Project in 1981, focusing on three components to develop an academic program with a Latino cultural context:

- Intensive English instruction in writing and reading about the students' Latino cultural experiences and identity
- Latino counselors who have first-hand knowledge of the challenges that students face
- Mentors from the Latino professional community

Students learn academic skills to help them succeed in college while they understand and value their cultural heritage. Counselors provide ongoing support to students and their parents as the students face the academic environment. Through relationships with academic and professional Latino mentors, students observe successful individuals who have not discarded their cultural identities. The program now enrolls approximately thirty students each year at thirty-nine California community colleges. All interested students may participate in the Puente Project, though most participants are Latino students.

The Puente Project offers a support system for underrepresented students to succeed academically while they preserve and value their cultural identity. The program simultaneously encourages students to build connections with the institution and maintain (and even strengthen) meaningful cultural influences, such as the family and other members of the Latino community. As such, the Puente Project meets Tinto's three criteria for effective retention programs.

The Puente Project includes and reaches beyond campus resources to foster a supportive network for students. By involving Latino community members who serve as mentors to underrepresented students, the Puente Project offers students positive examples of how others have successfully completed their educations and maintained their cultural identities. The statewide involvement in the Puente Project indicates a strong institutional commitment to student welfare.

Strategic Retention Initiatives

The dean for student affairs at a college at a highly selective, residential research-extensive university began several strategic initiatives to connect proactively with first-year students (Brier, 1999). The initiatives were designed with three goals in mind:

- Promote institutional affiliation among students (and their families)
- Identify at-risk students
- Connect students to available university resources

In a series of intentional outreach efforts, the dean aims to create meaningful dialogues with new students as soon as possible. Before summer orientation sessions with students and their families, the dean reads all students' application files. During the sessions, she makes selected, relevant references about students' interests in welcoming speeches and informal conversations with students and family members. After the semester begins, each first-year student receives a personal phone call from the dean sometime between the fourth and sixth week of fall classes. By this point of the semester, sufficient time has elapsed for students to experience academic and social challenges. The phone conversation focuses on what the student thinks about his or her academic and social experiences thus far at the university (their courses, living situations, and activities, for example). Through the brief conversations, students know that someone at the college cares about their particular experiences, and the dean can connect students with appropriate campus resources, such as tutors, student organizations, residence life staff, and the health center. Depending on the issues discussed, some students receive follow-up phone calls, some students schedule in-person appointments, and others have no further contact during the semester. During the beginning of the second semester, the dean calls each student again, referring to the notes of the initial conversation. Finally, each student receives a personally signed birthday card from the dean through campus mail to help celebrate the student's first birthday on campus.

Through repeated, intentional individual contacts with students, the dean interacts in an informed, personal manner. Students experience a pattern of supportive outreach efforts from someone in the institution who understands how the college works and who also knows them. Through these strategic initiatives, the dean can personify the values of the institution as caring and supportive of student success, a clear way to show institutional commitment to the welfare of students. The strategic initiatives meet Tinto's three criteria for effective retention programs.

Undergraduate Research Opportunity Program

Faculty-student research partnerships form the basis of the Undergraduate Research Opportunity Program (UROP) at the University of Michigan (Nagda and others, 1998). Started in 1989, UROP is open to all first-year and sophomore students, though it specifically targets underrepresented minority and women interested in the sciences. Partnership opportunities are available in most departments in the College of Literature, Science, and the Arts and in the professional schools, such as law, business, and medicine.

Students and faculty mutually select each other to form a partnership based on shared research interests. They meet during the academic year to develop a research project together. Coupled with the faculty mentoring relationship, UROP participants attend peer research interest groups led by students who have completed the program. The peer advisers support participants by sharing their experiences with UROP and by helping them develop their research projects. Students can earn academic credit through their participation in UROP.

The program meets all three of Tinto's criteria of effective programs and addresses many antecedents for social integration. By combining faculty and peer mentoring to expose students to research early in their academic careers, UROP supports new students in their transitions to the college community. Devoting such resources shows an institutional commitment to student welfare, and the peer interactions offer opportunities for communal potential and psychosocial engagement.

What the Exemplary Retention Programs Represent

The nine exemplary programs represent myriad types of retention efforts that reflect the institutional cultures and goals of the campus communities that created them. As such, they provide a variety of approaches to address issues of student persistence rather than optimal programs to be adopted whole cloth by other institutions. Offering enough details to understand the basic design of the programs, the descriptions show several methods of supporting student success. The nine programs vary in breadth and depth of scope (from a single office project to a statewide system program) and initiators (students, faculty, and administrators). The institutional settings of these projects include universities (public and private) and community colleges. Most initiatives

TABLE 1
Exemplary Retention Programs

Name of Program	Campus Initiators	Residential/ Commuter	Racial or Ethnic Minority Focus	Tinto's Criteria
Campus Retention Committee	Students	Either	Yes	1, 2, 3
College Process Review	Administrators	Either	No	1, 2, 3
Collegia Program	Administrators	Commuter	No	1, 3
C.L.A.S.S.	Administrators/ Students	Residential	Yes	1, 2, 3
Decision Tree	Administrators	Either	No	1, 2, 3
FAST Program	Faculty	Either	No	1, 2, 3
Puente Project	Administrators	Commuter	Yes	1, 2, 3
Strategic Retention Initiatives	Administrators	Either	No	1, 2, 3
UROP	Faculty	Either	Yes	1, 2, 3

are available to all interested students (Tinto's second principle), while some target subpopulations of students, such as commuters, residential students, and underrepresented racial or ethnic students (see Table 1). All have features that may be adapted to a variety of institutions, and all include elements that may positively influence social integration. Decisions regarding which approaches might work best for specific institutions should rest with the members of those communities who are informed about relevant research on student departure.

Reducing Institutional Rates of Departure

THIS CHAPTER OFFERS an overarching recommendation and a set of specific recommendations for institutional policy and practice that take the form of powerful levers of institutional action. We offer recommendations to reduce student departure for residential colleges and universities, commuter colleges and universities, and for racial or ethnic minority students. We do not present specific recommendations to guide policy and practice to reduce student departure at the level of state systems of higher education. Nevertheless, some recommendations may also apply at this level.

An Overarching Recommendation

We assert that institutional efforts to reduce student departure should use an integrated design approach. By integrated design, we mean that all institutional policies and practices developed to reduce student departure are intentional and require coordination to ensure that guidelines for the development of such policies and practices are steadfastly followed by designated institutional officers. An integrated design approach adheres to the following seven guidelines:

1. *Many small policy levers rather than one single policy lever should be developed.* Pascarella and Terenzini (1991, p. 655) contend that many small policy levers may be more effective in achieving an institutional goal than one single large-scale policy lever. The ill-structured nature of the problem of college student departure also suggests the use of multiple policy levers.

2. *The policies and practices developed should embrace one or more of Tinto's three principles of effective retention.* His first principle stipulates that institutions must espouse an enduring commitment to students served by the institution (Tinto, 1993, p. 146). His second principle ordains that an institution must be committed to the education of all its students. This commitment places importance on student learning. Effective retention programs strive to integrate all students into the social and academic communities of a college or university. Such programs encourage the development of personal bonds among students, faculty, administrators, and staff of the college or university. Such is Tinto's third principle of effective retention.

3. *The president, chief academic officer, and chief student affairs officer of an institution must embrace and support the policies and practices developed to reduce institutional departure.* The notion of the commitment of the institution to student welfare identified by Braxton and Hirschy (forthcoming) receives reinforcement in this guideline.

4. *All members of the college community need to have a stake in the success of policies and practices to reduce student departure.* Put differently, administrators, faculty, and staff members must demonstrate a commitment to the policies and practices developed. Their day-to-day actions and interactions with students should demonstrate such a commitment. The notion of institutional integrity delineated by Braxton and Hirschy (forthcoming) finds palpable expression in adherence to this guideline. Likewise, this guidelines bolsters commitment of the institution to the welfare of its students.

5. *Policies and practices should empower students to take responsibility for their own college success.* Several of the exemplary student retention programs involve students' taking the initiative to help themselves and their peers meet their educational goals. The Decision Tree program provides an example of students' responding to a caring offer made by college staff. Many retention programs feature peer support, including the Campus Retention Committee, C.L.A.S.S., and the FAST project.

6. *Some student departure may be in the best interest of the student or the institution* (Tinto, 1982). The reduction of unnecessary student departure should be the goal of policies and practices.

7. *Enacted policies and practices should be assessed for their effectiveness.* This guideline echoes our fourth general recommendation for further scholarship advanced in the previous chapter.

Powerful Institutional Levers of Action

The specific recommendations for policy and practice that we present in this section constitute many small levers of action directed toward the goal of reducing institutional student departure. We characterize these levers of action as powerful because they flow from research findings reviewed in this monograph and adhere to one or more of Tinto's three principles of effective retention (Braxton and Mundy, 2001–2002). Colleges and universities serious about reducing their rates of student departure should implement the vast majority of these recommendations. Moreover, the guidelines for an integrated design in policies and practices to reduce institutional departure should also be followed.

Braxton and Mundy (2001–2002) advance forty-seven recommendations that, they assert, hold promise for reducing institutional rates of student departure, as they follow one or more of Tinto's principles of effective retention and spring from research findings. These recommendations were derived from articles appearing in a special issue of *Journal of College Student Retention* (Braxton, 2001–2002) titled "Using Theory and Research to Improve College Student Retention." We present many of these recommendations offered by Braxton and Mundy and advance others derived from the literature and research findings reviewed in this volume. The findings of research reviewed in this volume also back the recommendations put forth by Braxton and Mundy. We present recommendations to foster student retention pertinent to residential colleges and universities, commuter colleges and universities, and to racial or ethnic minority students.

In addition to recommendations tailored for these different types of colleges and universities and for racial or ethnic minority students, we also offer recommendations that promote student retention in both residential and commuter colleges and universities. Put differently, the following recommendations pertain to both residential and commuter colleges and universities, whereas subsequent recommendations apply specifically to residential or commuter collegiate institutions.

Financial aid should be awarded to students demonstrating financial need. College and university administrators, faculty, and staff frequently view financial aid as an admissions recruitment tool. However, it also plays a significant role in the retention of students. Accordingly, Braxton and McClendon (2001–2002) stress that every effort should be made to award financial aid to each aid applicant that demonstrates financial need. They point out that applicants who demonstrate low levels of need should receive aid, as such individuals are frequently expected to secure the small amount of financial resources they need to attend a particular college or university. Satisfaction with the costs of attending a particular college or university result from such efforts. Braxton and Mundy (2001–2002) also recommend such institutional efforts. *Individual colleges and universities must make commitment to the welfare of their students an abiding concern.* The growth and development of its students, the high value placed on students as individuals and as members of groups, and the equal treatment and respect for the individual student constitute ways in which a college or university demonstrates commitment to the welfare of its students. We offer an array of recommendations that demonstrate an institution's commitment to the welfare of its students. These recommendations stem from two aspects of such a commitment: a concern for the growth and development of students, and the high value placed on students.

Student Growth and Development
The teaching practices of faculty play a significant role in fostering the growth and development of students. Accordingly, we offer the following specific recommendations:

Institutional policies and practices should encourage faculty members to improve on existing teaching methods and skills or to acquire new ones. Faculty development activities and the faculty reward system must stimulate faculty to refine or learn new teaching methods and skills. For example, faculty development workshops and seminars should concentrate on active learning techniques in general and cooperative/collaborative learning in particular. *Some positive weight in the faculty reward system (for example, reappointment, annual salary, tenure and promotion decisions) should be given to faculty members who use teaching methods that facilitate student retention* (Braxton and McClendon, 2001–2002; Braxton and Mundy, 2001–2002). *The assessment of faculty teaching role performance should include indices of the teaching skills of instructional clarity and organization and preparation as well as indices of active learning* (Braxton and McClendon, 2001–2002; Braxton and Mundy, 2001–2002).

Valuing Students

The high value placed on students, respect for the student as an individual, and the equal treatment of students receive reinforcement through the following recommendations:

The campus environment should be characterized by its fairness toward students (Berger, 2001–2002). Specifically, *rules and regulations governing student life should be enforced in a fair manner* (Braxton and McClendon, 2001–2002; Braxton and Mundy, 2001–2002). *Clear and effective lines of communication about the goals, values, policies, and procedures of the institution should be developed to keep students apprised of matters important to them* (Berger, 2001–2002; Braxton and McClendon, 2001–2002; Braxton and Mundy, 2001–2002). At a minimum, students should be kept informed of rules and regulations important to them. *Students should be given opportunities to participate in organizational decision making* (Berger, 2001–2002; Braxton and Mundy, 2001–2002). *Institutional integrity should be an enduring concern of the individual college or university.* As discussed elsewhere in this volume, a college or university that demonstrates a steadfast adherence to its stated mission and goals is an institution of high institutional integrity. The decisions and actions of the administrators, faculty, and staff of an institution determine the integrity of a given college or university (Braxton and Hirschy, forthcoming). Specifically, an institution can exhibit institutional integrity by following these two recommendations:

The mission of the college or university should function as a foundation for decision making and administrative action. Put differently, colleges and universities must be true to their missions by enacting policies and procedures congruent with the mission and goals of the institution (Kuh, 2001–2002).

Prospective student applicants must receive an accurate picture of the academic and social dimensions of a college or university. Specifically, recruitment activities and publications must accurately represent the institution. Moreover, prospective students should be encouraged to visit the campus (Braxton and McClendon, 2001–2002; Braxton and Mundy, 2001–2002).

Residential Colleges and Universities

The programs conducted in residential colleges and universities described in the previous chapter provide the basis for institutional actions to reduce student departure. In addition to the implementation of these programs, we offer recommendations that flow from three of the six possible sources of influence on social integration included in the revision of Tinto's interactionalist theory we presented earlier. Accordingly, we group the recommendations for reducing institutional rates of student departure in residential colleges and universities according to these three possible sources of influence on social integration. These sources of influence spring from research findings.

Communal Potential

As stated previously, communal potential finds expression as a student's perception that a subgroup of students with attitudes, values, beliefs, and goals similar to those of other students exists on campus. The following recommendations assist students in assessing whether they anticipate membership in such an affinity group or cultural enclave:

Orientation programs for first-year students should provide several opportunities for students to socially interact with their peers (Braxton and McClendon,

2001–2002; Braxton and Mundy, 2001–2002). *Residential colleges and universities should require all first- and second-year students to reside in a college or university residence hall.* Residence halls should also provide opportunities for social interaction among residents (Braxton and McClendon, 2001–2002; Braxton and Mundy, 2001–2002). *A sense of community should characterize each residence hall.* The method of assigning first-year students to residence halls should facilitate the development of a sense of community (Braxton and McClendon, 2001–2002; Braxton and Mundy, 2001–2002).

Proactive Social Adjustment

As indicated previously in this volume, students who adjust to college in proactive ways demonstrate this possible source of influence on social integration. More specifically, proactive social adjustments entail engagement in anticipatory socialization behaviors to ready oneself for college and the use of stress coping strategies that respond to stress in a positive way. The recommendations we advance strive toward helping students adjust to college in proactive rather than reactive ways.

To assist students in their anticipatory socialization efforts, we strongly recommend that *student participation in orientation programs for first-year students be mandatory.* By requiring participation in orientation, students engaged in anticipatory behaviors will have their needs met. Those students not prone toward anticipatory socialization behaviors will benefit from the information they receive through orientation activities.

Students can acquire a knowledge of various stress coping strategies. Students can learn proactive strategies, in particular. Accordingly, we suggest that *colleges and universities offer workshops to students on coping with stress* (Braxton and McClendon, 2001–2002; Braxton and Mundy, 2001–2002).

Psychosocial Engagement

As described elsewhere in this volume, psychosocial engagement pertains to the amount of psychological energy students expend in meeting new friends, participating in the social life of their college or university, and taking part in campus extracurricular activities. We highly recommend that colleges and universities develop ways to foster the involvement of students through participation in campus extracurricular activities, interactions with peers, and interactions with faculty members. Astin (1984, p. 298) maintains that the assessment of institutional policies and practices should focus on their effectiveness in increasing student involvement. Findings reviewed in this monograph give rise to this recommendation.

The crux of two previously advanced recommendations also foster psychosocial engagement in all students as well as meet the needs of students entering college with a well-developed desire to expend the needed psychological energy for engagement in the social communities of their college. These slightly altered recommendations are:

Orientation programs for first-year students should provide several opportunities during the academic year for students to socially interact with their peers (Braxton and McClendon, 2001–2002; Braxton and Mundy, 2001–2002). *Residence halls should provide multiple opportunities for social interaction among residents* (Braxton and McClendon, 2001–2002). Residence halls might also sponsor some extracurricular activities such as intramural athletic competition.

Commuter Colleges and Universities

In the previous chapter, we describe programs conducted in commuter colleges and universities. We urge commuter institutions to consider the implementation of one or more of these programs. We also proffer recommendations that stem from two sources of influence embedded in the theory of student departure we propose in the chapter "Student Departure in Commuter Colleges and Universities." These sources of influence are communities of learning and support from significant others for attending college.

Communities of Learning

In the theory of student departure from commuter colleges and universities we advance in this volume, communities of learning play a central role in the retention of students. Accordingly, we advance with great vigor the following recommendation:

Commuter colleges and universities should develop learning communities. As stated elsewhere in this volume, learning communities involve the block scheduling of courses so that the same students take several courses together. A theme usually undergirds these courses. Cooperative learning methods should be the primary method of instruction used in these courses. This recommendation stems from research by Tinto (1997).

Support from Significant Others

The support of parents, spouses, and friends plays a significant part in both the theory of student departure we advance in this volume and Bean and Metzner's conceptual model (1985). For some students enrolled in commuter institutions, this needed support already exists. For others, such support must develop. The recommendations we suggest seek to develop such needed support for college attendance by significant others. We present these recommendations in two categories: developing support from spouses/life partners and developing support from parents.

Developing Support from Spouses/Life Partners.   Support from spouses or life partners may develop if some stresses and burdens associated with college attendance lessen. The following recommendations aim to reduce the burdens or stresses placed on family life associated with college attendance.

Commuter colleges and universities should develop academic spaces and support service for commuter students. Such academic space and support services should include physical spaces for students to type papers, study, make copies, and print materials. Such spaces should be open to students in the evenings and on weekends. *Commuter colleges and universities should offer courses at a variety of times to accommodate the work schedules and family obligations of their students.* The availability of food services should match the times courses are offered (Andreas, 1983). To be sure, the vast majority of commuter institutions have flexible course offerings and food service hours. Nevertheless, college administrators and faculty must work together to ensure that sections of required courses are offered during the day and evening and on weekends to accommodate the needs of commuter students. *Commuter colleges and universities should develop on-campus employment opportunities for their students* (Rue and Ludt, 1983). On-campus employment alleviates some of the stress of commuting to school and going to work off campus. *Commuter colleges and universities should develop child-care services for their students.* The availability of drop-in day-care services would reduce some of the stress of having children and attending college. *Commuter colleges and universities should include spouses and life partners in the orientation programs for new students.* Programs for spouses and life partners should focus on information about the institution, the stresses associated with college attendance, and the availability of services designed to help commuter students.

Developing Parental Support. Adequate financial aid and the opportunity for on-campus employment serve to develop parental support for college attendance. Jacoby (1983) points out, however, that commuter institutions should forge parental identification with the institution. She notes that many students enrolled in commuter colleges and universities are first-generation college students. The parents of such students may question the value of college attendance. Consequently, the development of parental identification with the focal college may foster parental support for college attendance.

Identification with the college may develop through orientation programs for new students. Thus, we recommend:

Commuter colleges and universities should encourage parents to attend new student orientation. Such orientation programs should also include sessions designed to inform parents about the college and the stresses of college attendance (Jacoby, 1983).

Administrators, faculty, and staff of commuter colleges and universities should make parents feel welcome when they attend college functions. Parents, like students, should feel part of the college community.

Reducing the Departure of Racial or Ethnic Minority Students

The marked difference between the departure rates of racial or ethnic minority students in contrast to white students necessitates the development of approaches to reducing their departure rates. The recommendations offered above should foster the retention of students from racial or ethnic minority groups, but the difference in departure rates suggests the need for additional remedies. Accordingly, we offer the following recommendations.

Colleges and universities must enroll and retain a critical mass of racial or ethnic minority students. In particular, residential colleges and universities must enroll a sufficient number of minority students to ensure the formation of cultural enclaves or affinity groups comprised of such students. *Colleges and universities should embrace a diverse student body.* Embracing diversity should receive reinforcement by inviting speakers, holding programs, and conducting workshops that honor the history and cultures of different racial or ethnic groups on campus (Braxton and McClendon, 2001–2002; Braxton and Mundy, 2001–2002). *Colleges and universities should implement Tierney's intervention model for "at-risk students."* Tierney (2000) developed his model from research on college preparation programs. He posits that at-risk students are more likely to persist in college if they receive affirmation of their identities and experience incorporation into the cultures of their college or university. He proposes an intervention model based on this underlying assumption. Thus, we assert that colleges and universities should implement the model developed by Tierney to reduce the departure rate of such students. We encourage individuals interested in implementing this model to read the chapter titled "Power, Identity, and the Dilemma of College Student Departure" in *Reworking the Student Departure Puzzle* (Braxton, 2000c).

Although students from racial or ethnic minority groups enroll in both residential and commuter colleges and universities, some of the recommendations for practice we advance for commuter colleges and universities also apply, in full force, to such groups of college students. Those recommendations focusing on support from significant others seem particularly relevant. Support and involvement from the communities where such students reside is also of critical importance (Tierney, 2000).

Reductions in institutional rates of departure depend on the implementation of the recommendations we advance in this chapter by individual colleges and universities. Improvement in the collegiate experience for many college students depends on the efforts of scholars and practitioners concerned with the student departure puzzle.

Conclusions and Recommendations for Scholarship

THIS CHAPTER ADVANCES a set of conclusions derived from the research findings reviewed and the theoretical formulations advanced in this volume. We also offer a set of four general and eight specific recommendations for further scholarship on the college student departure process.

Conclusions

We advance a set of six conclusions.

As expressed in this volume, Tinto's interactionalist theory holds paradigmatic stature as an explanation for college student departure as indexed in the shear volume of citations to his work. The assessment of this theory (described earlier), however, seriously challenges the paradigmatic status of this theory. To elaborate, sociologist Robert Merton (1968) differentiated between grand and middle-range theory. Grand theory seeks to explain a wide range of phenomena, whereas middle-range theories endeavor to explain a limited range of phenomena. Braxton (2000b) states that college student departure is a limited phenomenon within the broader phenomenon of the college student experience. Nevertheless, he extends the distinction between grand and middle-range theories to capture the college student departure process. If Tinto's theory is a grand theory, then validity for his theory would result across different types of colleges and universities and different groups of students. A theory of the middle range, however, best depicts Tinto's interactionalist theory, as it partially accounts for student departure in residential colleges and universities but fails to account for student departure in commuter institutions. Moreover, only five of this theory's thirteen propositions receive strong empirical affirmation in residential collegiate institutions. *Thus, we conclude that scholars and practitioners should seriously question the paradigmatic stature of Tinto's interactionalist theory.* Instead, scholars and practitioners should focus on middle-range theories of college student departure.

In this volume, we advance theories of the middle range to explain college student departure. From a set of propositions derived from research findings, we formulate a theory to account for student departure from commuter colleges and universities. To explain departure in residential colleges and universities, we offer a revision of Tinto's theory. *Although both of these theories seek to explain departure in different types of colleges and universities, both of them include constructs reflective of economic, organizational, psychological, and sociological orientations toward student departure.* The ill-structured nature of the problem of college student departure necessitates such a multidisciplinary perspective (Braxton and Mundy, 2001–2002).

Both the revision of Tinto's theory to account for student departure in residential institutions and the theory of student departure in commuter institutions meet three criteria for a good theory suggested by Chafetz (1978). First, both theories advanced in this volume account for research findings about student departure. Second, the propositions of both theories lend themselves to empirical testing. Third, both theories are relatively parsimonious, as only propositions essential to account for research findings are included.

The structure of the college student experience includes two key dimensions: the academic and the social. Although the importance of the academic dimension to the college student experience transcends residential and commuter institutions and different types of students through its structured form (such as courses and degree requirements), the roles of academic and social dimensions in student departure differ substantially between these two types of colleges and universities. The theories presented in this volume depict such a contrast. *The academic dimension plays a significant role in the departure process in commuter institutions, whereas in residential colleges and universities, the social dimension performs a predominant role.*

An upper limit on the improvement of student retention rates in commuter colleges and universities exists. Structural characteristics of commuter institutions create such an upper limit. Laden, Milem, and Crowson (2000) note that higher rates of student departure occur at commuter institutions. They partially attribute such high departure rates to the lack of residentiality in commuter colleges and universities. Residentiality is more than residence halls; it is symbolic physical and social removal of students from membership and participation in their precollege everyday life (Kamens, 1977). The absence of residentiality results in weak or nonexistent social communities at commuter colleges and universities. Students with high needs for social affiliation will likely depart from a commuter institution, as satisfaction of this need will not likely occur. Likewise, students from college-educated families will also expect residentiality and well-defined social communities. Thus, second-generation college students will also likely depart from a commuter college or university. *Nevertheless, possible improvement in student retention rates in commuter colleges and universities depends on the creation of communities of learning.* Although it is important for institutional leaders to share what has worked on their campuses and consider successful programs at other schools, *no template of a successful retention program exists* (Hossler, 1991; Tinto, 1993). The review in the chapter "Exemplary Student Retention Programs" affirms this stance. As such, the complexity of the student departure process can be considered an ill-structured problem (Braxton and Mundy, 2001–2002). The ongoing exchange between researchers and practitioners will likely lead to both theoretical and practical insights that will serve students better. Institutional retention efforts that are both theoretically grounded and rooted in reflective practice offer the best potential for supporting students' educational goals.

Recommendations for Further Scholarship

We advance four general recommendations and ten more specific recommendations for further scholarship on the college student departure process. The implementation of these recommendations enables our understanding of college student departure to make substantial headway in the next decade of the seventy-year history of research on this puzzling phenomenon. Our general recommendations take the following form.

General Recommendations

Research on college student departure should continue to use constructs derived from economic, organizational, psychological, and sociological orientations. The ill-structured nature of the "departure puzzle" gives force to this recommendation.

Scholars conducting studies of the college student departure process should provide more detailed descriptions of the institutional setting for their studies. At a minimum, scholars should indicate whether the institution is a four-year or two-year residential institution, or a four-year or two-year commuter institution. The findings reviewed in this monograph make distinctions among four-year residential institutions, four-year commuter institutions, and two-year commuter colleges in the college student departure process. Some authors of studies, however, do not provide such needed information. Future research on college student departure depends on scholars' offering such institutional descriptions.

Multiple replications of tests of the theories of college student departure presented in this volume should occur to permit the type of theory assessment conducted by Braxton, Sullivan, and Johnson (1997). Replications of tests of theories presented of student departure presented elsewhere should also occur.

Pascarella (1986) maintains that policies and practices designed to reduce college student departure should be empirically appraised for their efficaciousness. We support his assertion. He suggests that institutional research officers might conduct such assessments. Braxton (1999) posits that reliable knowledge about effective policies and practices might result from such a program of research and development. However, the development of such a knowledge base depends on replications of policies and programs across different institutional settings, consistency in the measurement of core concepts related to theories of student departure, publication of the findings of such research and development activities in academic and professional journals, and description of efficacious policies and practice in sufficient detail to guide the implementation of the focal policy or practice at another college or university (Braxton, 1999).

Specific Recommendations

We advance the following eight specific recommendations.

Research testing the revision of Tinto's interactionalist theory posited in this volume should take place in a variety of residential colleges and universities. Such testing should occur in liberal arts colleges, comprehensive colleges and universities, and research universities. (Figure 5 on p. 30 graphically illustrates the theory to be tested.)

Empirical testing of the revision of Tinto's theory should focus on validity of this revised theory for different groups of college students. Does the magnitude of the influence of the constructs of ability to pay and communal potential differ between white students and racial or ethnic minority students?

Empirical testing of the theory of student departure in commuter colleges and universities postulated in this volume should occur in a variety of commuter colleges and universities. Specifically, such testing should take place in both two-year community colleges and four-year commuter institutions. (Figure 6 on p. 43 graphically portrays the theory to be tested.)

Empirical testing of the theory of student departure from commuter colleges and universities should focus on the validity of this theory for different groups of college students. Does the magnitude of the influence of the constructs of this theory vary between white students and racial or ethnic minority students?

Both the revision of Tinto's theory in residential collegiate institutions and the theory of student departure from commuter colleges and universities include commitment of the institution to student welfare and institutional integrity as influences on student departure decisions.

We recommend research focusing on the identification of factors that influence students' perceptions of the commitment of their institution to the welfare of its students and the integrity of their institutions. Specifically, we posit that the four models of organizational functioning described by Birnbaum (1988) may act as such possible sources of influence. The four models described by Birnbaum are the bureaucratic, collegial, political, and anarchical.

Birnbaum asserts that each model exists in every college or university but that one model predominates. Berger (2000b) calls these models organizational dimensions that define the environment of an organization. Different goals, values, and methods of decision making define each of these organizational dimensions. These organizational dimensions affect administrative action in various ways. These ways, in turn, affect the interpretations students make of their experiences with such administrators as the registrar, financial aid officers, student affairs officers, and academic deans. Such interpretations influence the perceptions of students concerning the commitment of their institution to student welfare and the integrity of institutional action.

We also posit that psychological environments or climates at the level of the college or university may also affect such student perceptions. Student perceptions of the environments of their college or university affect their behavior (Baird, 2000). Such behaviors, in turn, influence their interpretations of their collegiate experiences. Such judgments affect the perceptions students hold of their college or university. Friendliness, supportive and helpful, and intellectual constitute dimensions of the psychological climate that may shape student perceptions (Baird, 2000). Thus, these environmental dimensions may affect student views on the integrity of the actions of his or her institution and on the magnitude of the commitment of his or her institution to the welfare of its students.

Our revision of Tinto's interactionalist theory of student departure from residential colleges and universities identifies communal potential as an important source of influence on student social integration. Influences on communal potential include the existence of social fraternities and sororities on campus. In addition, the cultural capital possessed by a student may also shape his or her perceptions concerning the potential for community at his or her college or university.

Berger (2000a) extends Bourdieu's notion of cultural capital (1973, 1977) to account for student departure in general and social integration in particular. Cultural capital is symbolic and a type of knowledge valued by the elite members of society (McDonough, 1997). Habits, manners, styles of speech, educational credentials, and lifestyle preferences characterize cultural capital (Bourdieu, 1973, 1977). Social interactions among peers in the form of conversations about travel abroad and attending such cultural events as the symphony, the ballet, or a Broadway play signify the possession of cultural capital (Braxton, 2003).

Berger (2000a) maintains that both individual students and individual colleges and universities exhibit varying degrees of cultural capital. The likelihood of student persistence is greater if the student's level of cultural capital matches the level of cultural capital embedded in the social and organizational systems of a given college or university. We assert that perceptions of communal potential are also influenced by the degree to which student and institutional levels of cultural capital coincide. *We recommend research in residential colleges and universities that use these formulations.*

In addition to cultural capital, Kuh and Love (2000) offer eight propositions that relate student culture to the process of college student departure. The underlying thrust of these eight propositions focuses on the extent to which the student's culture of origin coincides with the culture of various student peer groups existing at a particular college or university. Tinto (1993) also views centrality and marginality as important determinants of student departure.

We alter two of the eight propositions to account for the shaping of communal potential: Propositions 4 and 5. First, the degree of communal potential is inversely related to the cultural distance between the student's culture of origin and the culture of immersion (Proposition 4). Thus, the smaller the cultural distance, the greater the degree of communal potential. Second, students who transverse a long cultural distance must acclimate themselves to the dominant cultures of immersion or join one or more cultural enclaves to perceive a sense of communal potential (Proposition 5). Put differently, such students are unlikely to experience a sense of communal potential if they are unable to acclimate themselves to the dominant culture or to join a cultural enclave. *We recommend the testing of these two altered propositions of Kuh and Love (2000) in future studies in residential colleges and universities.* The theory of student departure from commuter colleges and universities advanced in this volume identifies an important role for communities of learning. *We recommend research that delineates other aspects of the classroom that play a role in a student's decision to depart from a commuter college or university.* Research shows that the use of active learning practices by faculty (Braxton, Milem, and Sullivan, 2000) and such teaching skills as clarity, organization, and preparation (Braxton, Bray, and Berger, 2000) indirectly influence student departure from residential universities. Such aspects of teaching may also influence student departure from commuter colleges and universities. We suggest the inclusion of these teaching aspects in tests of the theory of student departure from commuter institutions advanced in this volume.

Although research on student departure is well represented in the literature (Fife and Barnett, 1986; Kezar, 1999; Mayville, 1989), gaps still exist. Because each college and university exists in a particular context (Hossler, 1991), *detailed case studies of institutional retention programs are needed to assist administrative and faculty colleagues in assessing the degree to which the programs might be applicable to another institutional setting.* Currently, program descriptions at liberal arts institutions and religiously affiliated institutions are sparse in the literature. Universities and community colleges are better represented, but many descriptions are only cursory.

Finally, professional associations can serve an integral role in collecting and disseminating resources about institutional retention programs. Such information should be formatted for easy access by campus leaders. Researchers and practitioners should continue to share descriptions of retention programs in place and offer reflections on the effectiveness of programs in practice so that the literature base continues to evolve.

Closing Thoughts

This monograph does not cover such topics as graduate student departure, the departure of lesbian and gay students, and departure from a state system of higher education. We invite other scholars to review literature and research on these important topics.

The history of research on college student departure spans more than seventy years. This span of time produced a theory that received paradigmatic stature, Tinto's interactionalist theory (1975, 1993), but a major conclusion of this volume challenges the paradigmatic stature of this theory. At best, Tinto's theory, with major revisions, is a theory of the middle range that accounts for student departure from residential institutions. We offer such a revision of Tinto's theory. We also advance a theory to explain student departure from commuter colleges and universities.

Progress in further understanding the college student departure puzzle depends on the willingness of scholars to carry out the recommendations for further scholarship advanced in this volume. If implemented, a deeper understanding of the student departure process between commuter and residential institutions as well as among different groups of college students will result.

Moreover, reductions in institutional rates of departure depend on the implementation of the recommendations we advance in this chapter by individual colleges and universities. Improvement in the collegiate experience for many college students depends on the efforts of scholars and practitioners concerned with the student departure puzzle.

References

Allen, D. F., and Nelson, J. M. (1989). Tinto's model of college withdrawal applied to women in two institutions. *Journal of Research and Development in Education, 22*(3), 1–22.

Alwin, D. F., and Otto, L. B. (1977). Higher school context effects on aspirations. *Sociology of Education, 50,* 259–273.

American Association of State Colleges and Universities. (1994). Campus practices for student success: A compendium of model programs. Washington, DC: American Association of State Colleges and Universities.

American College Testing Program. (2001). *ACT newsroom.* [http://www.act.org/news/releases/2001/charts.html]. Retrieved October 2002.

Anderson, M. S., and Louis, K. S. (1991). *Subscription to norms and counternorms of academic research: The effects of departmental structure and climate.* Paper presented at a meeting of the Association for the Study of Higher Education, October 21–November 3, Boston.

Andreas, R. E. (1983). Institutional self-study: Serving commuter students. In S. S. Stewart (Ed.), *Commuter students: Enhancing their educational experience.* New Directions for Student Services, no. 24. San Francisco: Jossey-Bass.

Arrington, P. G. (1994). *AASCU/Sallie Mae National Retention Project.* Washington, DC: American Association of State Colleges and Universities.

Astin, A. W. (1984). Student involvement: A developmental theory for higher education. *Journal of College Student Personnel, 25,* 297–308.

Attinasi, L. C., Jr. (1989). Getting in: Mexican Americans' perceptions of university attendance and the implications for freshman year persistence. *Journal of Higher Education, 60,* 247–277.

Attinasi, L. C., Jr. (1992). Rethinking the study of the outcomes of college attendance. *Journal of College Student Development, 33,* 61–70.

Baird, L. L. (1984). Relationships between ability, college attendance, and family income. *Research in Higher Education, 21,* 373–395.

Baird, L. L. (2000). College climate and the Tinto model. In J. M. Braxton (Ed.), *Reworking the student departure puzzle* (pp. 62–80). Nashville: Vanderbilt University Press.

Bandura, A. (1986). *Social foundations of thought and action: A social cognitive theory.* Englewood Cliffs, NJ: Prentice Hall.

Bandura, A. (1997). *Self-efficacy: The exercise of control.* New York: Freeman.

Bean, J. P., and Eaton, S. B. (2000). A psychological model of college student retention. In J. M. Braxton (Ed.), *Reworking the departure puzzle* (pp. 48–61). Nashville: Vanderbilt University Press.

Bean, J. P., and Metzner, B. S. (1985). A conceptual model of nontraditional student attrition. *Review of Educational Research, 55,* 485–540.

Berger, J. B. (1997). Students' sense of community in residence halls, social integration, and first-year persistence. *Journal of College Student Development, 38,* 441–452.

Berger, J. B. (2000a). Optimizing capital, social reproduction, and undergraduate persistence: A sociological perspective. In J. M. Braxton (Ed.), *Reworking the student departure puzzle* (pp. 95–126). Nashville: Vanderbilt University Press.

Berger, J. B. (2000b). Organizational behavior at colleges and student outcomes: A new perspective on college impact. *Review of Higher Education, 23,* 177–198.

Berger, J. B. (2001–2002). Understanding the organizational nature of student persistence: Empirically-based recommendations for practice. *Journal of College Student Retention, 3,* 3–22.

Berger, J. B., and Braxton, J. M. (1998). Revising Tinto's interactionalist theory of student departure through theory elaboration: Examining the role of organizational attributes in the persistence process. *Research in Higher Education, 39,* 103–119.

Berger, J. B., and Milem, J. F. (1999). The role of student involvement and perceptions of integration in a causal model of student persistence. *Research in Higher Education, 40,* 641–664.

Bers, T. H. (1985). Student major choices and community college persistence. *Research in Higher Education, 29,* 161–173.

Birnbaum, R. (1988). *How colleges work.* San Francisco: Jossey-Bass.

Bonwell, C. C., and Eison, J. A. (1991). *Active learning: Creating excitement in the classroom.* ASHE-ERIC Higher Education Report no. 1. Washington, DC: Graduate School of Education and Human Development, George Washington University.

Bourdieu, P. (1973). Cultural reproduction and social reproduction. In R. Brown (Ed.), *Knowledge, education, and cultural change* (pp. 189–207). London: Collier Macmillan.

Bourdieu, P. (1977). *Outline of a theory of practice* (R. Nice, Trans.). Cambridge, UK: University Press.

Braxton, J. M. (1999). Theory elaboration and research development: Toward a fuller understanding of college student retention. *Journal of College Student Retention, 1,* 93–97.

Braxton, J. M. (2000a). Introduction: Reworking the student departure puzzle. In J. M. Braxton (Ed.), *Reworking the student departure puzzle* (pp. 1–8). Nashville: Vanderbilt University Press.

Braxton, J. M. (2000b). Reinvigorating theory and research on the departure puzzle. In J. M. Braxton (Ed.), *Reworking the student departure puzzle* (pp. 257–274). Nashville: Vanderbilt University Press.

Braxton, J. M. (Ed.). (2000c). *Reworking the student departure puzzle*. Nashville: Vanderbilt University Press.

Braxton, J. M. (Ed.). (2001–2002). Using theory and research to improve college student retention [Special issue]. *Journal of College Student Retention, 3.*

Braxton, J. M. (2003). Persistence as an essential gateway to student success. In S. Komives and D. Woodard (Eds.), *Student services: A handbook for the profession* (4th ed.). San Francisco: Jossey-Bass.

Braxton, J. M., Bray, N. J., and Berger, J. B. (2000). Faculty teaching skills and their influence on the college student departure process. *Journal of College Student Development, 41,* 215–227.

Braxton, J. M., and Hirschy, A. S. (forthcoming). Modifying Tinto's theory of college student departure using constructs derived from inductive theory revision. In M. Yorke and B. Longden (Eds.), *Retaining students in higher education.* Buckingham, UK: Open University Press.

Braxton, J. M., and Lien, L. A. (2000). The viability of academic integration as a central construct in Tinto's interactionalist theory of student departure. In J. M. Braxton (Ed.), *Reworking the student departure puzzle* (pp. 11–28). Nashville: Vanderbilt University Press.

Braxton, J. M., and McClendon, S. A. (2001–2002). The fostering of social integration and retention through institutional practice. *Journal of College Student Retention, 3,* 57–72.

Braxton, J. M., Milem, J. F., and Sullivan, A. S. (2000). The influence of active learning on the college student departure process: Toward a revision of Tinto's theory. *Journal of Higher Education, 71,* 569–590.

Braxton, J. M., and Mundy, M. E. (2001–2002). Powerful institutional levers to reduce college student departure. *Journal of College Student Retention, 3,* 91–118.

Braxton, J. M., Sullivan, A. S., and Johnson, R. (1997). Appraising Tinto's theory of college student departure. In J. Smart (Ed.), *Higher Education: Handbook of Theory and Research* (Vol. 12, pp. 107–164). New York: Agathon.

Bray, N. J., Braxton, J. M., and Sullivan, A. S. (1999). The influence of stress-related coping strategies on college student departure decisions. *Journal of College Student Development, 40,* 645–657.

Brier, E. M. (1999). *Strategic initiatives.* Paper presented at a meeting of the Southern Graduate Student Association, New Orleans.

Cabrera, A. F., and others. (1999). Campus racial climate and the adjustment of students to college: A comparison between white students and African-American students. *Journal of Higher Education, 70,* 134–160.

Cabrera, A. F., Stampen, J. O., and Hansen, W. L. (1990). Exploring the effects of ability to pay on persistence in college. *Review of Higher Education, 13,* 303–336.

Carver, C. S., Scheier, M. F., and Weintraub, J. K. (1989). Assessing coping strategies: A theoretically based approach. *Journal of Personality and Social Psychology, 56,* 367–383.

Chafetz, J. S. (1978). *A primer on the construction and testing of theories in sociology.* Itasca, IL: F. E. Peacock.

Chickering, A. W., and Reiser, L. (1993). *Education and identity.* San Francisco: Jossey-Bass.

Christie, N. G., and Dinham, S. M. (1991). Institutional and external influences on social integration in the freshman year. *Journal of Higher Education, 62,* 412–436.

Cibik, M. A., and Chambers, S. L. (1991). Similarities and differences among Native Americans, Hispanics, Blacks, and Anglos. *NASPA Journal, 28,* 129–139.

Clark, B. R. (1972). The organizational saga in higher education. *Administrative Science Quarterly, 17,* 178–184.

Cofer, J., and Somers, P. (1999). An analytical approach to understanding student debtload response. *Journal of Student Financial Aid, 29*(3), 25–44.

Department of University Housing. (2002). *C.L.A.S.S. advocate job description.* [http://www.coe.uga.edu/echd/RA_files/ClassA.htm]. Retrieved December 2002.

Dolence, M. G. (1991). Setting the context for evaluation of recruitment and retention programs. In D. Hossler (Ed.), *Evaluating student recruitment and retention programs.* New Directions for Institutional Research, no. 70. San Francisco: Jossey-Bass.

Durkheim, E. (1951). *Suicide* (J. A. Spaulding and G. Simpson, Trans.). Glencoe, IL: Free Press.

Eaton, S. B., and Bean, J. P. (1995). An approach/avoidance behavioral model of college student attrition. *Research in Higher Education, 36,* 617–645.

ERIC Clearinghouse for Community Colleges. (2000, October). *Retention programs in the community colleges: Topical bibliography.* [http://www.gseis.ucla.edu/ERIC/bibs/Retention.htm]. Retrieved December 2002.

ERIC Clearinghouse on Higher Education. (2002a, January). *Critical issue bibliography sheet (CRIB): Early intervention.* [http://www.eriche.org/crib/early.html]. Retrieved December 2002.

ERIC Clearinghouse on Higher Education. (2002b, January). *Critical issue bibliography sheet (CRIB): Hispanic students.* [http://www.eriche.org/crib/hispanic.html]. Retrieved December 2002.

ERIC Clearinghouse on Higher Education. (2002c, January). *Critical issue bibliography sheet (CRIB): Native American college students.* [http://www.eriche.org/crib/native%20american%20college%20students.html]. Retrieved December 2002.

ERIC Clearinghouse on Higher Education. (2002d, January). *Critical issue bibliography sheet (CRIB): Retention and recruitment of underrepresented faculty and students.* [http://www.eriche.org/crib/retention.html]. Retrieved December 2002.

ERIC Clearinghouse on Higher Education. (2002e, January). *Critical issue bibliography sheet (CRIB): Summer bridge programs.* [http://www.eriche.org/crib/bridge.html]. Retrieved December 2002.

Erwin, T. D. (1983). The scale of intellectual development: Measuring Perry's scheme. *Journal of College Student Personnel, 24,* 6–12.

Fife, J. D., and Barnett, L. (1986). *Emerging trends in higher education.* Washington, DC: ERIC Clearinghouse on Higher Education. (ED 276 367)

Gaither, G. H. (Ed.). (1999). *Promising practices in recruitment, remediation, and retention.* New Directions for Higher Education, no. 108. San Francisco: Jossey-Bass.

Hagedorn, L. S., Maxwell, W., and Hampton, P. (2001–2002). Correlates of retention for African-American males in community colleges. *Journal of College Student Retention, 3,* 243–263.

Halpin, R. L. (1990). An application of the Tinto model to the analysis of freshman persistence in a community college. *Community College Review, 17,* 22–32.

Heath, D. (1980). Wanted: A comprehensive model of healthy development. *Journal of Personnel and Guidance, 58,* 391–399.

Helland, P. A., Stallings, H. J., and Braxton, J. M. (2001–2002). The fulfillment of expectations for college and student departure decisions. *Journal of College Student Retention, 3,* 381–396.

Heverly, M. A. (1999). Predicting retention from students' experiences with college processes. *Journal of College Student Retention, 1,* 3–11.

Holland, B. (1997). Analyzing institutional commitment to service: A model of key organizational factors. *Michigan Journal of Community Service Learning, 4,* 30–41.

Hossler, D. (Ed.). (1991). *Evaluating student recruitment and retention programs.* New Directions for Institutional Research, no. 70. San Francisco: Jossey-Bass.

Hossler, D., Braxton, J. M., and Coopersmith, G. (1989). Understanding student college choice. In J. C. Smart (Ed.), *Higher education: A handbook of theory and research* (Vol. 5). New York: Agathon.

Hu, S., and St. John, E. P. (2001). Student persistence in a public higher education system: Understanding racial and ethnic differences. *Journal of Higher Education, 72,* 265–286.

Jacoby, B. (1983). Parents of dependent commuters: A neglected resource. In S. S. Stewart (Ed.), *Commuter students: Enhancing their educational experience.* New Directions for Student Services, no. 24. San Francisco: Jossey-Bass.

Kaltenbaugh, L. S., St. John, E. P., and Starkey, J. B. (1999). What difference does tuition make? An analysis of ethnic differences in persistence. *Journal of Student Financial Aid, 29*(2), 21–31.

Kamens, D. H. (1977). Legitimating myths and educational organization: The relationship between organizational ideology and formal structure. *American Sociological Review, 42,* 208–219.

Kezar, A. (1999). *Higher education trends (1997–99): Students.* Washington, DC: ERIC Clearinghouse on Higher Education. (ED 435 353)

Kitchener, K. (1986). The reflective judgment model: Characteristics, evidence, and measurement. In R. Mines and K. Kitchener (Eds.), *Adult cognitive development.* New York: Praeger.

Kuh, G. D. (2001–2002). Organizational culture and student persistence: Prospects and puzzles. *Journal of College Student Retention, 3*(1), 23–39.

Kuh, G. D., and Love, P. G. (2000). A cultural perspective on student departure. In J. M. Braxton (Ed.), *Reworking the student departure puzzle: New theory and research on college student retention* (pp. 196–212). Nashville: Vanderbilt University Press.

Laden, B. V. (1998). An organizational response to welcoming students of color. In J. S. Levin (Ed.), *Organizational change in the community college: A ripple or a sea change?* New Directions for Community Colleges, no. 102. San Francisco: Jossey-Bass.

Laden, B. V., Milem, J. F., and Crowson, R. L. (2000). New institutional theory and student departure. In J. M. Braxton (Ed.), *Reworking the student departure puzzle* (pp. 235–256). Nashville: Vanderbilt University Press.

Maldonado, D., Rhoads, R. A., and Chang, G. (2002). *The student-initiated retention project: Toward a theory of student self-empowerment.* Paper presented at a meeting of the Association for the Study of Higher Education, November, Sacramento.

Mangold, W. D., and others. (2002–2003). Who goes, who stays: An assessment of the effect of a freshman mentoring and unit registration program on college persistence. *Journal of College Student Retention, 4,* 95–122.

Mayville, Z. (1989). *Emerging trends in higher education.* Washington, DC: ERIC Clearinghouse on Higher Education. (ED 317 109)

McDonough, P. (1997). *Choosing colleges: How social class and schools structure opportunity.* Albany: State University of New York Press.

McGrath, P., and Galaviz, F. (1996). In practice: The Puente project. *About Campus, 1*(5), 27–30.

Merton, R. K. (1968). *Social theory and social structure.* New York: Free Press.

Milem, J. F., and Berger, J. B. (1997). A modified model of college student persistence: Exploring the relationship between Astin's theory of involvement and Tinto's theory of student departure. *Journal of College Student Development, 38,* 387–400.

Miller, G. D. (1994). Predicting freshmen persistence and voluntary withdrawal from Heath's model of maturing. Unpublished dissertation, Syracuse University.

Murdock, T. A. (1987). It isn't just money: The effects of financial aid on student persistence. *Review of Higher Education, 11,* 75–101.

Mutter, P. (1992). Tinto's theory of departure and community college student persistence. *Journal of College Student Development, 33,* 310–318.

Nagda, B. A., and others. (1998). Undergraduate student-faculty research partnerships affect student retention. *Review of Higher Education, 22,* 55–72.

Newcomb, T. M. (1966). The general nature of peer group influence. In T. M. Wilson and E. K. Wilson (Eds.), *College peer groups: Problems and prospects for research* (pp. 2–16). Chicago: Aldine.

Nora, A. (1987). Determinants of retention among Chicano college students: A structural model. *Research in Higher Education, 26,* 31–59.

Nora, A. (1990). Campus-based aid programs as determinants of retention among Hispanic community college students. *Journal of Higher Education, 61,* 312–331.

Nora, A., Attinasi, L. C., and Matonak, A. (1990). Testing qualitative indicators of precollege factors in Tinto's attrition model: A community college perspective. *Review of Higher Education, 13,* 337–356.

Nora, A., Cabrera, A. F., Hagedorn, L. S., and Pascarella, E. (1996). Differential impacts of academic and social experiences on college-related behavioral outcomes across different ethnic and gender groups at four institutions. *Research in Higher Education, 37,* 427–451.

Okun, M. A., Benin, M., and Brandt-Williams, A. (1996). Staying in college: Moderators of the relation between intention and institutional departure. *Journal of Higher Education, 67*, 577–596.

Olivas, M. A. (1986). Financial aid and self-reports by disadvantaged students: The importance of being earnest. *Research in Higher Education, 25*, 245–252.

Pascarella, E. T. (1986). A program of research and policy development in student persistence at the institutional level. *Journal of College Student Personnel, 27*, 100–107.

Pascarella, E. T., and Chapman, D. W. (1983). Validation of a theoretical model of college withdrawal: Interaction effects in a multi-institutional sample. *Research in Higher Education, 19*, 25–48.

Pascarella, E. T., and Terenzini, P. T. (1991). *How college affects students.* San Francisco: Jossey-Bass.

Pascarella, E. T., Terenzini, P. T., and Wolfle, L. M. (1986). Orientation to college and freshman year persistence/withdrawal decisions. *Journal of Higher Education, 57*, 155–175.

Pavel, D. M. (1991). *Assessing Tinto's model of institutional departure using American Indian and Alaskan Native longitudinal data.* Paper presented at a meeting of the Association for the Study of Higher Education, October 31–November 3, Boston.

Pike, G. R., Schroeder, C. C., and Berry, T. R. (1997). Enhancing the educational impact of residence halls: The relationship between residential learning communities and first-year college experiences and persistence. *Journal of College Student Development, 38*, 609–621.

Porter, O. F. (1990). *Undergraduate completion and persistence at four-year colleges and universities: Detailed findings.* Washington, DC: National Institute of Independent Colleges and Universities.

Rue, P., and Ludt, J. (1983). Organizing for commuter student services. In S. S. Stewart (Ed.), *Commuter students: Enhancing their educational experience.* New Directions for Student Services, no. 24. San Francisco: Jossey-Bass.

St. John, E. P. (1991). A framework for reexamining state resource-management strategies in higher education. *Journal of Higher Education, 62*, 263–287.

St. John, E. P., Cabrera, A. E., Nora, A., and Asker, E. H. (2000). Economic influences on persistence reconsidered: How can finance research inform the reconceptualization of persistence models? In J. M. Braxton (Ed.), *Reworking the student departure puzzle* (pp. 29–47). Nashville: Vanderbilt University Press.

St. John, E. P., Kirschstein, R. J., and Noell, J. (1991). The effects of student financial aid on persistence: A sequential analysis. *Review of Higher Education, 14*, 383–406.

St. John, E. P., and Noell, J. (1989). The effects of student financial aid on access to higher education: An analysis of progress with special consideration of minority enrollment. *Research in Higher Education, 30*, 563–581.

St. John, E. P., Paulsen, M. B., and Starkey, J. B. (1996). The nexus between college choice and persistence. *Research in Higher Education, 37*, 175–220.

St. John, E. P., and Starkey, J. B. (1995). An alternative to net price: Assessing the influence of prices and subsidies on within-year persistence. *Journal of Higher Education, 66*, 156–186.

Schmitz, D. (2002). *A "home away from home" for commuter students: The Seattle University Collegia Program.* [http://www.naspa.org]. Retrieved December 2002.

Schuh, J. H. (1999). Examining the effects of scholarships on retention in a fine arts college. *Journal of College Student Retention, 1,* 193–202.

Schwartz, S. A. (1990). *Application of a conceptual model of college withdrawal to technical college students.* Paper presented at a meeting of the American Education Research Association, April, Boston.

Sewell, W. H., Haller, A. O., and Portes, A. (1969). The educational and early occupational attainment process. *American Sociological Review, 34,* 82–92.

Sewell, W. H., and Hauser, R. M. (1975). *Education, occupation, and earnings: Achievement in early career.* New York: Academic Press.

Sewell, W. H., and Shah, V. P. (1978). Social class, parental encouragement, and educational aspirations. *American Journal of Sociology, 3,* 559–572.

Sieveking, N., and Perfetto, G. (2000–2001). A student-centered individual-level university retention program where attrition is low. *Journal of College Student Retention, 2,* 341–353.

Solberg, V. S. (1993). Development of the college stress inventory for use with Hispanic populations: A confirmatory analytic approach. *Hispanic Journal of Behavioral Sciences, 15,* 490–497.

Somers, P., Cofer, J., Below, D., and Freeman, T. (2002). *Persistence of students of color at two-year colleges.* Paper presented at the Annual Forum of the Association for Institutional Research, April, Toronto, ON.

Stampen, J. O., and Cabrera, A. F. (1986). Exploring the effects of student aid on attrition. *Journal of Student Financial Aid, 16*(2), 28–40.

Stern, G. (1970). *People in context: Measuring person-environment congruence in education and industry.* New York: Wiley.

Stewart, S. S., and Rue, P. (1983). Commuter students: Definition and distribution. In S. S. Stewart (Ed.), *Commuter students: Enhancing their educational experiences.* New Directions for Student Services, no. 24. San Francisco: Jossey-Bass.

Stodt, M. M., and Klepper, W. M. (Eds.). (1987). *Increasing retention: Academic and student affairs administrators in partnership.* New Directions for Higher Education, no. 60. San Francisco: Jossey-Bass.

Strauss, A., and Corbin, J. (1990). *Basics of qualitative research: Grounded theory procedures and techniques.* London: Sage.

Taylor, J. D., and Miller, T. K. (2002). Necessary components for evaluating minority retention programs. *NASPA Journal, 39,* 266–283.

Thompson, C. E., and Fretz, B. R. (1991). Predicting the adjustment of black students at predominantly white institutions. *Journal of Higher Education, 62,* 437–450.

Tierney, W. G. (2000). Power, identity, and the dilemma of college student departure. In J. M. Braxton (Ed.), *Reworking the student departure puzzle* (pp. 213–234). Nashville: Vanderbilt University Press.

Tinto, V. (1975). Dropout from higher education: A theoretical synthesis of recent research. *Review of Educational Research, 45,* 89–125.

Tinto, V. (1982). Limits of theory and practice in student attrition. *Journal of Higher Education, 53,* 687–700.

Tinto, V. (1986). Theories of student departure revisited. In J. Smart (Ed.), *Higher education: A handbook of theory and research* (Vol. 2, pp. 359–384). New York: Agathon.

Tinto, V. (1987). *Leaving college: Rethinking the causes and cures of student attrition.* Chicago: University of Chicago Press.

Tinto, V. (1993). *Leaving college: Rethinking the causes and cures of student attrition* (2nd ed.). Chicago: University of Chicago Press.

Tinto, V. (1997). Classrooms as communities: Exploring the educational character of student persistence. *Journal of Higher Education, 68,* 599–623.

Tinto, V. (1998). Colleges as communities: Taking research on student persistence seriously. *Review of Higher Education, 21,* 167–177.

Tinto, V. (2000). Linking learning and leaving. In J. M. Braxton (Ed.), *Reworking the departure puzzle* (pp. 81–94). Nashville: Vanderbilt University Press.

U.S. Department of Education. (2002). *Digest of education statistics, 2001* (NCES 2002–130). Washington, DC: U.S. Government Printing Office.

Voorhees, R. A. (1985). Student finances and campus-based financial aid: A structural model analysis of the persistence of high-need freshmen. *Research in Higher Education, 22,* 65–92.

Voorhees, R. A. (1987). Toward building models of community college persistence: A logit analysis. *Research in Higher Education, 26,* 115–129.

Wallace, W. (1971). *The logic of science in sociology.* Chicago: Aldine Atherton.

Webb, M. W., II. (1990). *Development and testing of a theoretical model for predicting student degree persistence at four-year commuter colleges.* Paper presented at a meeting of the American Educational Research Association, April, Boston.

Wilcox, L. (1991). Evaluating the impact of financial aid on student recruitment and retention. In D. Hossler (Ed.), *Evaluating student recruitment and retention programs.* New Directions for Institutional Research, no. 70. San Francisco: Jossey-Bass.

Wood, P. (1983). Inquiring systems and problem structure: Implications for cognitive development. *Human Development, 26,* 249–265.

Zhang, Z., and RiCharde, R. S. (1998). *Prediction and analysis of freshman retention.* Paper presented at the Annual Forum of the Association for Institutional Research, May, Minneapolis.

Name Index

Solberg, V. S., 50
Somers, P., 37, 50
St. John, E. P., 28, 32, 37, 50
Stallings, H. J., 24
Stampen, J. O., 22, 27, 37
Starkey, J. B., 32, 37, 50
Stern, G., 39
Stewart, S. S., 44
Stodt, M. M., 54
Strauss, A., 22
Sullivan, A. S., 1, 2, 7, 9–18, 25, 30, 41, 42, 82, 86

T

Terenzini, P. T., 23, 25, 45, 67
Thompson, C. E., 25
Tierney, W. G., 77, 78

Tinto, V., 2, 3, 7–11, 13–20, 23, 28, 29, 32, 35, 36, 38–42, 44, 45, 49, 50, 54, 55, 68, 75, 81, 85, 87

V

Voorhees, R. A., 37, 38

W

Wallace, W., 21
Webb, M. W., II, 44
Weintraub, J. K., 25, 26
Wilcox, L., 54
Wolfle, L. M., 23, 25

Z

Zhang, Z., 38, 39

Subject Index

---

and Decision Tree, 60–61
and Freshmen Academic Support and
  Tracking Program, 61–62
and Puente Project, 62–63
selecting exemplary, 54–56
sources of, 53–54
and Strategic Retention Initiatives,
  63–64
three principles for assessing, 55
and Undergraduate Research
  Opportunity Program, 64–65
Reworking the Student Departure Puzzle
  (Braxton), 2, 77

S

Significant others, support from, 40, 75
Social adjustment, proactive, 24–26
Social integration, influences on, 21–28
Sociological influences, 39–41
Sociological orientation, 29
Spouses, developing support from,
  75–76
Strategic Retention Initiatives, 63–65
Student departure
  guidelines for reducing, 67–69
  ill-structured problem of, 1–4
  powerful institutional levers of action for
    reducing, 69–72

reducing institutional rates of, 67–78
and student growth and development,
  70–71
and valuing students, 71–72
Student welfare, commitment of institution
  to, 22–33

T

Two-year colleges, 17–18

U

Undergraduate Research Opportunity
  Program (UROP; University of
  Michigan), 62, 64–65
U.S. Department of Education, 3
University of Arkansas, 61
University of California, Los Angeles, 56
University of Michigan, 62
University of Wisconsin, 37
UROP program
  See Undergraduate Research
    Opportunity Program
"Using Theory and Research to Improve
  College Student Retention"
  (Braxton and Mundy), *69*

V

Vietnamese students, 56

About the Authors

John M. Braxton is professor of education in the Higher Education Leadership and Policy Program in the Department of Leadership, Policy, and Organizations at Peabody College, Vanderbilt University. His research interests center on the college student experience, the sociology of the academic profession, and academic course-level processes. He has published more than sixty refereed journal articles and book chapters on topics related to these areas of research interest. His current scholarly interests include research and theory development pertaining to college student departure, scientific misconduct, and the normative structure of undergraduate college teaching.

Braxton also has edited three books: *Reworking the Student Departure Puzzle* (Vanderbilt University Press), *Perspectives on Scholarly Misconduct in the Sciences* (Ohio State University Press), and *Faculty Teaching and Research: Is There Conflict?* (Jossey-Bass). He is also the coauthor of two books. With Alan E. Bayer, Braxton wrote *Faculty Misconduct in Collegiate Teaching* (Johns Hopkins University Press), and with William Luckey and Patricia Helland, he wrote *Institutionalizing a Broader View of Scholarship Through Boyer's Four Domains* (ASHE-ERIC Higher Education Report, vol. 29, no. 2, Jossey-Bass).

Amy S. Hirschy served as a college student services administrator for thirteen years before returning to graduate study. Grounded in practical experience at small private colleges and large state universities, Hirschy now studies higher education issues, works as a research assistant, and serves as a peer mentor for teaching assistants at Vanderbilt University in Nashville, Tennessee. Her research interests include the college student experience in general and, more specifically, factors that positively and negatively influence students' educational persistence. Hirschy and her coauthor, Maureen E. Wilson, received the Betty L. Harrah award for the manuscript of the year for their article, "Walking the Thin Line: The Challenges of Policy Enforcement for Resident Assistants" in the *Journal of College and University Student Housing*. Braxton and Hirschy recently collaborated on a chapter in *Retention and Student Success in Higher Education* (Open University Press).

Shederick A. McClendon is an assistant professor of higher education administration in the Department of Education Policy, Research, and Administration at the University of Massachusetts at Amherst. His research interests include education leadership, policy, and equity. His research emphasizes the factors that influence college student experiences and retention. Most recently, he served as a research associate at the Tennessee Higher Education Commission and taught undergraduate courses at Vanderbilt University, where he is completing his Ph.D. in higher education leadership and policy. He holds an M.P.H. from the University of Pittsburgh and a B.S. in biology from Morehouse College.

About the ASHE-ERIC Higher Education Reports Series

Since 1983, the ASHE-ERIC Higher Education Report Series has been providing researchers, scholars, and practitioners with timely and substantive information on the critical issues facing higher education. Each monograph presents a definitive analysis of a higher education problem or issue, based on a thorough synthesis of significant literature and institutional experiences. Topics range from planning to diversity and multiculturalism, to performance indicators, to curricular innovations. The mission of the Series is to link the best of higher education research and practice to inform decision making and policy. The reports connect conventional wisdom with research and are designed to help busy individuals keep up with the higher education literature. Authors are scholars and practitioners in the academic community. Each report includes an executive summary, review of the pertinent literature, descriptions of effective educational practices, and a summary of key issues to keep in mind to improve educational policies and practice.

The Series is one of the most peer reviewed in higher education. A National Advisory Board made up of ASHE members reviews proposals. A National Review Board of ASHE scholars and practitioners reviews completed manuscripts. Six monographs are published each year and they are approximately 120 pages in length. The reports are widely disseminated through Jossey-Bass and John Wiley & Sons, and they are available online to subscribing institutions through Wiley InterScience (http://www.interscience.wiley.com).

Call for Proposals

The ASHE-ERIC Higher Education Report Series is actively looking for proposals. We encourage you to contact the editor, Dr. Adrianna Kezar, at kezar@usc.edu with your ideas. For detailed information about the Series, please visit http://www.eriche.org/publications/writing.html.

Recent Titles

Volume 30 ASHE-ERIC Higher Education Reports

1. Governance in the Twenty-First Century: Approaches to Effective Leadership and Strategic Management
   Dennis John Gayle, Bhoendradatt Tewarie, and A. Quinton White, Jr.
2. Retaining Minority Students in Higher Education
   Watson Scott Swail with Kenneth E. Redd and Laura W. Perna

Volume 29 ASHE-ERIC Higher Education Reports

1. Ensuring Quality and Productivity in Higher Education:
   An Analysis of Assessment Practices
   Susan M. Gates and Associates
2. Institutionalizing a Broader View of Scholarship Through Boyer's Four Domains
   John M. Braxton, William Luckey, and Patricia Helland
3. Transforming the Curriculum: Preparing Students for a Changing World
   Elizabeth A. Jones
4. Quality in Distance Education: Focus on On-Line Learning
   Katrina A. Meyer
5. Faculty Service Roles and the Scholarship of Engagement
   Kelly Ward
6. Identity Development of Diverse Populations: Implications for Teaching and Administration in Higher Education
   Vasti Torres, Mary F. Howard-Hamilton, Diane L. Cooper

Volume 28 ASHE-ERIC Higher Education Reports

1. The Changing Nature of the Academic Deanship
   Mimi Wolverton, Walter H. Gmelch, Joni Montez, and Charles T. Nies
2. Faculty Compensation Systems: Impact on the Quality of Higher Education
   Terry P. Sutton, Peter J. Bergerson
3. Socialization of Graduate and Professional Students in Higher Education:
   A Perilous Passage?
   John C. Weidman, Darla J. Twale, Elizabeth Leahy Stein
4. Understanding and Facilitating Organizational Change in the 21st Century: Recent Research and Conceptualizations
   Adrianna J. Kezar
5. Cost Containment in Higher Education: Issues and Recommendations
   Walter A. Brown, Cayo Gamber
6. Facilitating Students' Collaborative Writing
   Bruce W. Speck

Back Issue/Subscription Order Form

Copy or detach and send to:
Jossey-Bass, A Wiley Imprint, 989 Market Street, San Francisco CA 94103-1741

Call or fax toll-free: Phone 888-378-2537 6:30AM – 3PM PST; Fax 888-481-2665

Back Issues: Please send me the following issues at $24 each
(Important: please include series abbreviation and issue number.
For example AEHE 28:1)

_____

_____

_____

$ _____   **Total for single issues**

$ _____   SHIPPING CHARGES: SURFACE   Domestic Canadian
                                   First Item $5.00 $6.00
                                   Each Add'l Item $3.00 $1.50
                For next-day and second-day delivery rates, call the number listed above.

Subscriptions   Please ❏ start ❏ renew my subscription to *ASHE-ERIC Higher Education Reports* for the year 2_____at the following rate:

U.S.	❏ Individual $165	❏ Institutional $165
Canada	❏ Individual $165	❏ Institutional $225
All Others	❏ Individual $213	❏ Institutional $276
Online Subscription		❏ Institutional $165

**For more information about online subscriptions visit
www.interscience.wiley.com**

$ _____   Total single issues and subscriptions (Add appropriate sales tax for your state for single issue orders. No sales tax for U.S. subscriptions. Canadian residents, add GST for subscriptions and single issues.)

❏Payment enclosed (U.S. check or money order only)
❏VISA ❏ MC ❏ AmEx ❏ #_____ Exp. Date _____

Signature _____ Day Phone _____
❏ Bill Me (U.S. institutional orders only. Purchase order required.)

Purchase order # _____
                Federal Tax ID13559302   **GST 89102 8052**

Name _____

Address _____

_____

Phone _____ E-mail _____

For more information about Jossey-Bass, visit our Web site at www.josseybass.com

PROMOTION CODE ND03

ASHE-ERIC HIGHER EDUCATION REPORT IS NOW AVAILABLE ONLINE AT WILEY INTERSCIENCE

What is Wiley InterScience?

Wiley InterScience is the dynamic online content service from John Wiley & Sons delivering the full text of over 300 leading scientific, technical, medical, and professional journals, plus major reference works, the acclaimed Current Protocols laboratory manuals, and even the full text of select Wiley print books online.

What are some special features of Wiley InterScience?

Wiley Interscience Alerts is a service that delivers table of contents via e-mail for any journal available on Wiley InterScience as soon as a new issue is published online.
Early View is Wiley's exclusive service presenting individual articles online as soon as they are ready, even before the release of the compiled print issue. These articles are complete, peer-reviewed, and citable.
CrossRef is the innovative multi-publisher reference linking system enabling readers to move seamlessly from a reference in a journal article to the cited publication, typically located on a different server and published by a different publisher.

How can I access Wiley InterScience?

Visit http://www.interscience.wiley.com.

Guest Users can browse Wiley InterScience for unrestricted access to journal Tables of Contents and Article Abstracts, or use the powerful search engine.
Registered Users are provided with a *Personal Home Page* to store and manage customized alerts, searches, and links to favorite journals and articles. Additionally, Registered Users can view free Online Sample Issues and preview selected material from major reference works.
Licensed Customers are entitled to access full-text journal articles in PDF, with select journals also offering full-text HTML.

How do I become an Authorized User?

Authorized Users are individuals authorized by a paying Customer to have access to the journals in Wiley InterScience. For example, a University that subscribes to Wiley journals is considered to be the Customer. Faculty, staff and students authorized by the University to have access to those journals in Wiley InterScience are Authorized Users. Users should contact their Library for information on which Wiley journals they have access to in Wiley InterScience.

ASK YOUR INSTITUTION ABOUT WILEY INTERSCIENCE TODAY!